Canoeing and Kayaking

INSTRUCTION MANUAL

by Laurie Gullion

American Canoe Association

Menasha Ridge Press
Birmingham, AL

The American Canoe Association (ACA), founded in
1880, continues today as the oldest national canoeing
organization in the world, and one of the oldest national
sports governing bodies in North America.

The ACA is dedicated to water safety and to the promo-
tion of the various forms of canoeing as sport and recreation. Through its National Activities Committees, the
ACA sanctions and governs flatwater and whitewater
canoe and kayak racing in the United States. The
National Instruction Committee of the American Canoe
Association develops the guidelines for canoesport
instruction in the United States.

Contributions are deductible for income tax purposes.

Co-published by:

American Canoe Association
7432 Alban Station Boulevard
Suite B-226
Springfield, VA 22150
(703) 451-0141
www.acanet.org

Menasha Ridge Press
P. O. Box 43673
Birmingham, AL 35243
(800) 247-9437
www.menasharidge.com

Library of Congress Catalog Card Number 87-70837
ISBN 0-89732-136-7

Cover photo: Alan Fortune
Photo credits: Alan Fortune and James Swedburg

Printed in the United States.
Distributed by the Globe Pequot Press

ACKNOWLEDGEMENTS

Author Laurie Guillion is an outdoor educator and an instructor trainer for the American Canoe Association.

Editor Thomas Foster is former chairman of the ACA's National Instruction Committee and an ACA instructor trainer. He is the founder of the Outdoor Centre of New England, Inc., in Millers Falls, MA.

Layout, cover design and illustrations are by Carol A. Moore.

The ACA's *Canoeing and Kayaking Instruction Manual* has been developed under the direction of the National Instruction Committee.

The NIC gives special thanks to the following people for their advice and comments: William Endicott, U.S. Slalom Team Coach; Mac Thornton, Canoe Cruisers of America; Ogden Doremus, ACA Judicial Committee; Linda Harrison, Hampshire College; Ray McLain, NIC Member at Large.

TABLE OF CONTENTS

INTRODUCTION

Chapter I

Purpose

This manual is designed to help paddlers become knowledgeable, effective instructors and to assist experienced instructors in continuing their education.

The intent is to present the technical knowledge, paddling skills and teaching methods recommended by the American Canoe Association (ACA). The effort is an integral part of the ACA's comprehensive program for the development of canoesport.

As the internationally-recognized governing body for canoesport in the United States, the ACA through its National Instruction Committee is committed to the education of paddling instructors and the general public. Because paddling is a dynamic sport, the NIC strives to develop an awareness of safe, modern paddling and to promote the sharing of current thinking in the field.

The manual is a part of that process. It is one of many resources that instructors can use to create their own programs. The NIC recognizes that each instructor possesses a unique teaching style and works with participants who differ widely in their needs and abilities. The manual is intended to be an informational source from which instructors select material appropriate to the needs of their students.

While the manual reflects recent changes in canoesport, the NIC also recognizes that the material is subject to subsequent improvements. Instructors are encouraged to remain apprised of current information through the use of a variety of resources. The NIC will use *The American Canoeist* newsletter to provide periodic updates.

The techniques described in the manual are the essense of paddling at any level.

Format

The manual is organized into chapters that address:
1. safety
2. general technical information
3. specific paddling skills
4. a variety of teaching methods
5. elements of paddling lessons
6. specific ACA requirements in the instructor certification process

The three levels of courses developed by the ACA's National Instruction Committee are also addressed:
1. flatwater
2. moving water
3. whitewater

The suggested content for each ACA course at each level is outlined in the manual and reflects recent revisions by the NIC. Also, strokes and maneuvers for each type of craft are illustrated in two comprehensive chapters.

Types of Paddling

The manual addresses ACA courses in three major areas:
1. open canoeing, including solo (OC-1) and tandem (OC-2)
2. closed (or decked) canoeing (C-1 and C-2)
3. kayaking (K-1)

Paddlers from the sea kayaking community have requested assistance from the ACA in developing instructional workshops and in establishing a format for certifying instructors. The sea kayaking program is expected to be implemented by 1988.

The ACA is interested in promoting an awareness of canoesport in general and the interrelationship between all types of paddling. While each discipline has areas of difference, many shared elements are the foundation of all types of paddling. The ACA encourages instructors and participants in paddling programs to understand the similarities and to experience the differences.

A Call for Action

The ACA asks its instructors to continue their education as paddlers and teachers, because the rapidly-changing nature of canoesport demands it. An increased awareness of the biomechanical nature of sports in general has contributed to a greater understanding of the technical nature of canoesport.

The number of participants in the sport is growing, and they are increasingly knowledgeable consumers who are demanding responsible, professional instruction. In addition, all paddlers have a responsibility to promote safety in a potentially hazardous activity and to understand the current safety standards.

The alarming increase in fatalities among experienced paddlers also demands that all paddlers examine the factors that contributed to the accidents. All paddlers should take action to promote safety in canoesport.

The Value of Instructor Certification

Certification provides a forum for developing skilled instructors who are committed to modern instruction. Certification also helps to acquaint paddlers with generally accepted guidelines for paddling instruction. As a result, it establishes a measure of competency that protects participants, instructors and the activity itself.

The ACA's goal since its inception in 1880 is "education, not regulation." With the increasing popularity of paddling in general, the goal of education becomes even more important to maintain the integrity of the sport. Paddling has become more visible and more easily available to the public, and consequently, more people are participating. With the public's sometimes limited knowledge of safety and rescue skills, the likelihood of accidents increases. Tragic consequences, such as more drownings, are probable. Newcomers to the sport need a good introduction that encourages the development of their technical skills and knowledge.

Certification provides an avenue for paddlers to become acquainted with responsible, well-thought-out paddling programs. By participating in the certification process, paddlers are exposed to current trends in the sport and to the teaching methods of other instructors. As the recognized governing body for canoesport in the United States, the American Canoe Association brings people together to continue to improve skills in paddling and teaching through carefully assembled training programs.

Certification also provides paddlers with the ability to develop their sport in a meaningful way. Regulation by an external authority further removed from the field, like the federal or state government, is avoided. With its national base, the ACA enables paddlers to regulate themselves with input from the paddling community and to control the direction of the sport more strongly.

The certification process exposes paddlers to general criteria for instruction, but it also encourages instructors to seek a diversity of opinion to continue developing their programs.

SAFETY

Chapter II

Safety First!

Canoesport is a challenging, adventurous activity with inherent risks that make it an exciting sport. People are drawn to the sport for a variety of reasons: the thrill of playing in big waves, a long-distance tour through a chain of windy, remote lakes, the challenge of negotiating rocky rapids, a tour on a cold, spring day.

A primary goal of paddling instruction is to help students develop an awareness of safety issues in paddling and to develop the necessary skills that promote safe paddling. We need to educate the public about safety skills as well as technical paddling skills. The basis of solid paddling is safety awareness, and safety must come first in instruction.

Canoesport is a rapidly growing part of outdoor adventure education in which risk-taking is an accepted component. Individuals have the right to take calculated risks, and the ACA is committed to helping them handle those risks by becoming well-prepared, informed paddlers.

Outdoor adventure is defined by educators as a self-initiated activity in a natural setting that contains elements of real or apparent danger where the outcome, often uncertain, is affected by the actions of the participants and circumstance. As stated at the 1985 National Outdoor Recreation Trends Symposium, the object is *NOT* to eliminate the risk but to manage it at an acceptable level.

With the dramatic increase in canoesport's popularity has come an increase in accidents and fatalities. Accidents are usually the result of ignorance, and the majority of small craft fatalities each year involve unknowledgeable boaters. All paddlers need to examine these accidents and reaffirm their commitment to safety in the sport.

The Statistics Say It Best

Private and public agencies like the U.S. Coast Guard have profiled accidents to understand the common ingredients in boating fatalities. The public can learn from the mistakes of other boaters.

Examination of these accidents reveals five recurring problems:

1. *Paddlers are not wearing personal flotation devices.* Life jackets are either forgotten or used as padding. The lifejackets are often found floating near a swamped craft or trailing after the boat as it floats downriver.

2. *Cold water or cold weather is present.* Many accidents occur in the spring, especially during the freshet period. One typical scenario is a spring weekend with warm, sunny weather, high water levels and cold water. Often, paddlers are not dressed properly for the numbing effects of cold water. Drownings are often caused by hypothermia, where exposure to cold water and weather inhibits the ability of paddlers to rescue themselves.

3. *The victims are inexperienced.* Most fatalities involve inexperienced paddlers who have had no formal instruction or practice. The United States is generally a nation of self-taught paddlers who often do not understand the risks involved in canoesport, particularly in whitewater. However, an alarming increase in fatalities among skilled paddlers is occurring, although the total deaths are still fewer than those involving inexperienced paddlers.

4. *Alcohol is a contributing factor.* Many victims are drunk at the time of the accident. Drugs and canoesport do not mix. Drugs affect the coordination and judgment of

paddlers who need to respond quickly and intelligently in the face of hazards.

BE READY TO SWIM

"Cartoon by Dean Norman"

LOOK SHARP!
WEAR A LIFE VEST.

"Cartoon by Dean Norman"

DON'T LET WARM WEATHER CATCH YOU OFF-GUARD

CHECK WATER TEMP. BEFORE YOU FALL IN!

DON'T LET DRINKING LEAD TO TROUBLE

"Cartoon by Dean Norman"

SAVE THE BOTTLED FUN FOR *AFTER* THE RUN!

KNOW BEFORE YOU GO

"Cartoon by Dean Norman"

AVOID SURPRISES:

WHEN IN DOUBT STOP AND SCOUT

This poster series is a safety service of the American Canoe Association prepared through a U.S. Coast Guard grant. The series is available from the ACA National Office, P.O. Box 248, Lorton, VA 22079.

5. *The victims are often non-swimmers.* A look at the swimming histories of drowning victims shows that they have limited or no swimming ability. The ability to be at ease on or about water increases the ability to perform well in stressful situations. However, strong swimmers have also encountered problems because of the other factors.

Concern among paddlers is growing over the increasing number of skilled paddlers who die in boating accidents. The number of deaths among experienced paddlers has risen from one or two a year to *four in one weekend* in 1986. The increase is cause for the paddling community to explore the factors that contributed to these deaths.

The ACA's River Safety Task Force has examined those accidents since 1976 in two excellent but sobering publications available through the ACA Bookservice, *The Best of the River Safety Task Force Newsletter,* volumes I and II. Several alarming trends in the accidents are cause for concern:

1. *Misrepresentation of ability can lead to paddlers attempting rapids too difficult for their skills.* Paddlers can move very quickly today through the progression of instruction. Often, the result is that they suffer gaps in experience, especially in self-rescue or in recovery from potentially dangerous pinning situations. Paddlers are attempting more difficult rapids earlier in their development when they are less able to understand what can go wrong on the river and how to respond.

2. *The nature of a familiar run or rapid has been altered by changing environmental factors.* Complacency with a rapid paddled many times in the past can lead to problems in reacting quickly to unexpected changes. Fluctuating water levels (from rain or dam releases) can drastically affect the character of a river, just as hazards like toppled trees can create new dangers.

3. *Equipment affects a paddler's ability to perform safely.* Higher-performance equipment that is new to boaters can hinder their ability to paddle as effectively. Paddlers need a practice period in which to develop the necessary skill and comfort with new equipment.

Inadequate equipment can also affect a paddler's performance. The lack of full flotation or adequate walls (in decked boats) can make recovery from a capsize difficult or impossible.

4. *An inadequate support party can limit the effectiveness of rescue operations in an accident.* In whitewater, paddling alone or in parties of fewer than three boats is not recommended. Paddling in a group increases the safety of all participants, since more people can offer the security of swift and efficient rescues.

Instruction can help to promote safety in the sport. Students need to acquire the skills that enable them to take direct action to insure their own safety. They should understand that they are responsible for their own personal safety and for helping others in their paddling group.

The issue of proper judgment is one which all paddlers should address. Instructors can help in their lessons by raising questions concerning potential problems of judgment. For instance, these examples address situations with potential problems:

- A good friend who hasn't paddled recently may not be ready to attempt a familiar "neighborhood" rapid.
- No one else wants to scout the rapid, but one person has the nagging feeling that he should.
- A "friend of a friend" misrepresented his ability, and he may not be able to handle the river run chosen for the day.
- Someone forgot his lifejacket.

From the beginning, paddlers should analyze their abilities frankly and resist external pressure in making personal judgments about whether to paddle or portage a particular drop. It is an individual's ultimate responsibility to decide the best course of action for his own safety, and students should be encouraged to err on the side of safety throughout their entire paddling career. Newcomers are generally more inclined to listen to safety guidelines, but it is also important for experienced paddlers to remember those safety considerations.

Elements of Safety in Instruction

Prevention of accidents is the key to promoting safety in instruction. An instructor should consider the following variables in safe learning environments:

1. *Personal assumption of risk.* Students should understand the inherent hazards in the activity and realize that instructors cannot guarantee their safety. Students should assume responsibility for their own actions and realize that their actions affect the outcome of situations which may develop in the activities. They are ultimately responsible for their decision to participate in any paddling activity and their own safety.

2. *An orientation to basic safety guidelines in canoesport.* Students should understand the underlying tenets of safety in the sport. (*The American Whitewater Affiliation Safety Code* is one reference.) Appropriate clothing, equipment, group organization, and river running practices are a necessary part of a paddler's education.

3. *An orientation to self-rescue procedures that are the foundation of every rescue in canoesport.* Students must have an understanding of their individual responsibilities in the event of a capsizing. They must take direct action to insure their safety. Self-rescue procedures should be practiced from the outset, and individuals should understand that the ability of other rescuers to help them is affected directly by their ability to initiate a self-rescue.

4. *A thoughtful progression of activities.* Instructors must develop a progression of activities that leads to well-grounded skills. The activities should be designed to suit the abilities of the least experienced or least able paddler in the group. The progression can begin with a comfortable introduction on flatwater and moving water, where paddlers obtain a foundation in basic skills. With that experience, they will gain skills that help them to adjust to whitewater.

5. *A suitable physical environment.* Weather and the choice of terrain is a key safety factor. Air and water temperatures, wind and precipitation affect a paddler's ability to function efficiently on water. Classroom sites should also suit the student's abilities.

6. *Contingency plans for rescues and emergencies.* Instructors should be able to execute emergency procedures to rescue or evacuate injured or ill paddlers. The group should be prepared to deal with the possibility of emergencies with appropriate safety equipment and a reasonable knowledge of rescue techniques.

Paddling programs have the potential to expose an instructor to legal liability in the event of an accident that leads to an injury. An instructor should consider liability insurance for guided trips or instructional programs. The ACA offers an insurance policy to its certified instructors and instructor trainers for programs registered with the National Office.

INSTRUCTION

Learning is the process through which people acquire *skills* and *knowledge*. The acquisition of skills involves an improvement in physical and mental abilities, while the acquisition of knowledge refers to the gaining of new facts and ideas.

In examining instruction, the focus cannot be upon how instructors teach. Instead, the primary emphasis of this chapter will be an exploration of how people learn. It will also examine the components of a successful learning environment for the individual.

Learning through Doing

Modern theory says that learning occurs best through an integrated, coordinated use of many senses - hearing, seeing and doing. The most effective way to acquire new skills and knowledge is to experience the activity. The more senses involved, the better the learning that takes place.

Simultaneous use of many senses strengthens the learning process. By learning movement through sensation (as opposed to thinking about it), individuals will be able to retain the skills and knowledge longer and recall them more quickly. Ask superb paddlers how they improved their skills, and their answer is "by doing" - doing lots of paddling and doing it with other good paddlers who serve as models.

Frequent repetition of a physical skill develops "kinesthetic awareness." Simply stated, participants are acquiring "a *feel*" for the activity. To develop that kinesthetic sense, individuals must experience the movement to truly understand it. From the experience, they gain insight that enables them to ask meaningful questions and seek further information. They are fully involved in the process of learning.

Extended appeals to the ears (through lecture) or to the eyes (through demonstrations) will inhibit a person's ability to learn. When instructors "intellectualize" the approach, the direct experience is shortened and the students' development of sensitivity to the physical endeavor is hindered. In physical skill development, "doing" must be the largest part of a program for participants to learn effectively.

The emphasis on "learning through doing" represents a change in educational approach. Here is an explanation of the philosophy behind the change.

Learning through Adventure

Paddling is an adventurous sport undertaken in many arenas: on whitewater, on windy lakes, on flatwater in remote or wilderness areas. It is a challenging activity that requires participants to respond quickly and accurately to elements of real or apparent danger.

The important role that adventure can play in education has been well-documented because of its successful use in many outdoor education programs. Paddling programs are often cited as an integral part of adventure education because they are an excellent vehicle for individuals to experience directly the results of their actions.

The learning goals of adventure programs have been established clearly by Project Adventure Inc. in Hamilton, Massachusetts. Its goals, outlined below, are an example of what adventure-based programs strive to develop. The goal is helping the individual to:

1. *Experience a sense of increased self-worth.* A solid progression of activities enables people to see themselves as capable and competent.

2. *Develop improved coordination, agility and flexibility.* Balance, rhythm and timing are the basis of every physical activity, and their importance cannot be overlooked by an instructor.

3. *Become aware of the outdoors and respect it, not fear it.* The experience is often stressful for individuals unfamiliar with this new environment, but a successful program helps them to understand the outdoors.

4. *Find pleasure in using one's body and brain and sharing that pleasure with others.* The program must have an atmosphere of fun that enables and encourages an individual to make mistakes and learn from them.

Adventure activities involve taking risks within guidelines that minimize the danger. Participants need to accept the challenge in the sport and take responsibility for handling themselves. They need a program of activities that begins at a basic level and progresses in a manner that increases the likelihood of meeting the above goals.

Factors that Affect Learning

People vary in how they learn best, because many factors affect learning.

Age. Children have a well-developed kinesthetic awareness that enables them to learn a physical skill more easily than adults. Children are also more willing to make mistakes in an attempt to learn a skill. Adults, however, are sometimes more concerned with their image and are more easily embarassed by their mistakes. Because adults often have less kinesthetic awareness of their bodies, an instructor may have to help older students "feel" the skill by physically guiding their bodies through the movements.

Physical Characteristics. Participants' size, strength, and conditioning will affect their ability to learn. The nature of the skills or the length of the program has to be adjusted to meet the physical development and fitness level of the participants.

Fitness is often the limiting factor in developing new paddling skills. Encouraging an exercise program *in preparation* for a paddling class will increase participants' enjoyment and success in learning new skills.

Age, strength, physical fitness and personality are major factors that determine the manner in which people learn most effectively.

Intellectual Development. Adults often have strong preferences for teaching methods and are more resistant than children to new ideas in teaching. Adults who have been away from formal education may be nervous or ill-at-ease with planned programs; others may be uncomfortable with a games-oriented approach and prefer a more "serious" program.

Personality. Attitude, motivation and self-confidence will affect the ability to perform. Reluctant children may be signed up for lessons at the insistence of an adult. Adults are more often self-motivated. People new to physical activities need support to develop confidence in the ability to learn new skills.

Learning theories are varied, but educators generally agree that learning is enhanced by:

Repetition. Practice increases an individual's ability to learn. "Practice makes perfect" is an often repeated phrase, but a more accurate statement is that "perfect practice makes perfect." Accurate feedback is an integral part of improving through practice.

Association or progression. Information or experiences that people already possess lay a foundation for the learning of new skills and knowledge. Prior knowledge also affects the manner in which people learn. Understanding a student's background helps to relate those prior experiences to new material being introduced.

Motivation. People who want to learn or who understand the worth of an endeavor will learn more easily. Students can be motivated by many things, and with the students' help, instructors should strive to understand what is important to each individual.

Motivation to Learn

Instructors need to examine *why* students are seeking instruction to understand their wants and needs, and students need to share their reasons with instructors. Once instructors learn *what* is motivating each individual, then they can better tailor the instruction to the individuals. Successful instruction is a cooperative venture.

Participant "Wants"

Fun!!!. Enjoyment is an important consideration, and it is often affected by other "wants."

Safety. Danger is an inherent element in challenge/adventure activities, but participants do not want to be exposed to high degrees of risk.

Psychological Comfort. Intimidation can undermine the ability to learn, and participants want a supportive learning environment.

Fundamental Skills. Participants want to learn basic skills at their level of ability, and they want to feel that they can achieve those fundamentals.

Success. Participants want to experience the satisfaction of accomplishment.

Participant "Needs"

Instructor Competency. Participants need a capable instructor to help provide a successful learning experience without a high degree of risk and without relying upon the instructor as a guarantor of their safety.

Direction. Participants need an instructor to direct activities in a manner that helps them to learn fundamental skills successfully.

Physical Comfort. Participants need terrain that enhances their physical comfort. They also need to be dressed properly for the activity.

Participants must constantly evaluate their own needs which may change during an instructional program. Voicing their needs, concerns and what they believe to be the best course of action for themselves will help instructors develop a successful learning environment.

Individual Differences in Learning

People differ in how they involve various senses in their learning. The order in which they use the senses will also vary.

For example, some individuals need to listen to explanations before they experience an activity. Others need to watch a demonstration first. Still others need to feel the activity before they can begin to understand it.

Educators often characterize students in the following ways:

The Thinker (also known as the Technician) uses an analytical approach. The person often reads about the sport before doing it and needs technical explanations before beginning to acquire a skill. The mental process is initially more important than the physical, and more oral information is usually sought.

A close relative of the Thinker is the Talker. This person needs to repeat information to increase understanding of the activity. Be ready to minimize excessive talking and encourage the person to actually try the activity.

The Thinker

The Doer (also known as the Natural Mimic) uses a practical approach to learning, where the physical experience is more important than the mental process. This person wants only a quick demonstration of a skill before practicing it.

A close relative of the Doer is the Fidgeter. This person has a very short attention span during explanations and demonstrations and needs to be active to learn.

The Watcher likes to see the whole picture before attempting it. This person is often the last in line to try something and needs to reflect upon demonstrations and explanations of the activity.

A close relative of the Watcher is the Analyzer. This person becomes overly analytical and gets bogged down in reviewing other people's performances as well as his own.

The Feeler has a very strong awareness of physical movements and whether a motion is efficient or inefficient, similar or dissimilar to a demonstrated move. Sensory awareness is high, and analytical skills may be low.

Students in a lesson learn differently. Effective instructors recognize the differences and use a variety of teaching styles to meet their students' needs.

Teaching Styles

Instructors should vary their teaching styles to suit the manner in which individuals learn best. A mix of teaching styles generally works well in teaching groups.

Modern theory has identified these major styles:

Command. The instructor determines the subject matter, directs exercises and makes decisions about the lesson. This more authoritative style centers attention upon the instructor.

Task. The instructor explains a particular task, usually demonstrates it and then asks students to perform it. This style allows for more participation and individual decision-making in terms of the intensity and duration of participation.

Reciprocal. One person performs a task while a partner observes the performance, and then the pair switches roles. This style involves more analysis of a skill through two means: feeling the exercise and watching it. Small groups can also assume the roles which is often more comfortable for individuals who don't like to "stand out."

Guided Discovery. The instructor uses questions or exercises to lead a student to a desired result. The emphasis is upon students doing an activity and reaching their own conclusions based upon their experiences.

Problem Solving. The instructor introduces a problem and students are encouraged to explore a variety of solutions in their preferred manner. They can be asked to determine the best solution based upon their experiments.

The challenge in instruction is finding the teaching style that matches the students' needs. Being able to draw upon activities from all styles is an important consideration.

Characteristics of an Effective Instructor

Instructors should have the following qualifications:

Knowledge of Canoesport. Thorough knowledge is essential, particularly an awareness of trends and changes. The process is one of continuing education, where instructors should paddle with others, attend "update" clinics and remain in contact with other knowledgeable individuals.

Program Organization. An instructor is responsible for efficient organization of a lesson plan and the overall execution of the program, including equipment logistics and travel arrangements. The lesson plan involves a meaningful progression of activities that avoids a high degree of risk.

Ability to Model Effective Technique. The ability to demonstrate effective paddling skills is a necessity. Instructors should be able to demonstrate skills at a level higher than students. Demonstrations are often accompanied by a concise narration that explains the underlying skills of each maneuver. An ability to model technique in slow motion is important so that a skill can be broken down into component parts.

Leadership Ability and Judgment. Every paddling program should be conceived thoughtfully and executed responsibly by the instructor. Instructors must be able to take charge of difficult situations which may arise on water while realizing that many events are not in their control.

Physical Setting. Weather and terrain can affect learning, and participants should be properly protected from cold weather and water. Sheltered practice sites on lakes and rivers can lessen the frustration of learning new skills. Instructors should choose river sections that do not overwhelm a paddler's abilities. The difficulty of the water can be increased when a paddler is able to handle it safely.

Avoid shouting across noisy rapids, and talk "with" the wind. Choose practice areas that allow participants to rest in eddies and converse with partners and the instructor.

Equipment. Organize all classroom materials, handouts and program equipment, including paddling gear, prior to the start of the program. All equipment should be in good condition.

Develop a checklist for paddling equipment that matches the nature of the program. Remote or wilderness-style programs may require additional gear. Generally an instructor organizes:

Boats	Rescue bags or lines
Paddles	Lifejackets
First Aid Kit	Helmets
Equipment required by state or federal regulations	
Additional warm, dry clothing	

Facilities and Meeting Sites. If possible, choose sites that offer an area to warm up participants (shelters, parking area nearby for vehicles, public facilities). Contact a "host" site in advance to confirm arrangements for a program. Familiarize yourself with a new teaching environment prior to the workshop. Obtain the permission of private landowners to cross their properties. Respect the rights of other people (like the fishing community) to those sites.

Choose protected "classroom" sites. Windy areas frustrate paddlers and prevent them from developing a "feel" for the effects of their strokes.

Basic Instructional Methods

A basic teaching method involves three parts: demonstration, explanation and practice.

Demonstration is essential to teaching physical skills so that participants can watch and analyze efficient technique. An instructor's demonstration may occur at a normal pace or in slow motion to illustrate the various parts of a specific technique.

Avoid lengthy demonstrations that bore students. Some paddlers value demonstrations more highly after they have practiced the technique, because their increased understanding through experience will enable them to analyze the technique more closely.

A demonstration of inefficient technique is often an effective means of illustrating common problems. Demonstrations from different angles (front view or side view) offer greater understanding.

Demonstration and explanation often occur simultaneously so that a narration can help to underscore components of technique.

Explanation of the demonstration is necessary to encourage greater understanding of the demonstrated techniques. The intent is to draw attention to the more important components of the technique without becoming too technical. Keep the explanations simple.

Team teaching - where one instructor performs a skill and the other instructor provides commentary - is effective in providing good demonstrations and explanations.

Keep a class active and enthusiastic! Lengthy explanations can inhibit a paddler's ability to learn. Provide technical information simply and concisely throughout paddling practice.

Practice is an integral part of skill-building, because it encourages coordinated movement. Paddle handling or "sensitivity" is developed, and proper body positions are reinforced. Practice takes time, and people often need a warm-up period and frequent reviews to perform new skills smoothly.

Practice allows participants to refine their skills, especially when an instructor provides immediate feedback to reinforce the practice. Once the paddler performs the skill without thinking about it, then the purpose of practice has been realized. Developing efficient technique is exhilarating and students need enough practice time to experience that feeling.

The more traditional approach to teaching established this sequence: demonstration first, then explanation and finally practice. Increasingly, skilled instructors are discovering that reversing the process is a more effective way for participants to learn.

If an environment that encourages self-discovery is established, participants will find that actively experiencing new movements is very revealing and exciting. Because they discovered that themselves, they will be more likely to ask enlightened questions, to seek constructive solutions, and to be motivated to continue "doing." The paddler that is fully involved in the learning process from the beginning often progresses further than those who are less involved.

Fundamental Skills vs. Maneuvers

Individuals need to learn how to paddle efficiently, but the initial emphasis must be on fundamental skills rather than maneuvers. If basic skills are practiced first, then that repetition leads to an increased chance of succcess in mastering the maneuvers. Fundamental skills provide a foundation for the execution of maneuvers. If the process is abbreviated, then a student's maneuvers may be poorly executed.

Fundamental skills in paddling include:

- balance — a centered, relatively upright body
- boat lean — weight transfer through knee pressure, foot pressure and hip snaps
- basic body mechanics — efficient use of the lower body and upper body for boat lean and stroke execution
- paddling strokes — for power, turning and bracing
- coordination and fluidity — smoothness in technique where the body and craft function as one unit
- timing — in executing strokes, particularly in tandem craft

Maneuvers refer to:

- paddling in a straight line, forward and reverse
- eddy turns
- peelouts
- ferries
- spins
- slideslips or shifts
- surfing

Different Approaches to Practice

Instructors can use three basic approaches outlined in the American Red Cross instructor manual to help students understand paddling skills.

The Whole Approach asks the student to perform the whole technique at one time and works well for simple skills. Some people learn quickly using the whole approach and others have difficulty as the skills become more complex.

The Progressive-Part Approach allows students to practice the easiest part of the skill first, before they learn the next step in the sequence. As each new step is introduced, the participant learns the new part and then practices it in relation to the previous steps. If students have difficulty with one step, then they have repeated opportunities to practice the troublesome part in moving onto new steps.

The Part-Whole Approach focuses on each separate part of the technique and then practices all parts together. This method works best for students who can learn only one step at a time, but it may hold back quick learners who can grasp the overall technique easily.

An effective instructor watches to see which approach works best for each participant and adjusts the lesson to suit individual needs. Instructors may find that they need to ask students which approach is most beneficial and when. All three approaches may be used at different times in a program as the complexity of skills increases.

Changing a planned approach may be necessary if a student is encountering difficulty with a skill. In addition, instructors can avoid the boredom often associated with using one approach continually by responding to the satisfying challenge of creating a new program for each student.

LESSON ORGANIZATION

Chapter IV

Elements of a Teaching Progression

The National Instruction Committee recommends that instructors use these elements in their paddling lessons:

1. Orientation to paddling
2. Introduction of paddling strokes
3. Practice of paddling maneuvers
4. River practice site with moving water
5. River trip with multiple whitewater practice sites

Crucial to learning new skills is a progression of activities that encourages students to develop solid skills. The varying needs of students will affect the nature of the progression.

Generally, flatwater practice has the advantage of promoting a non-threatening atmosphere where paddlers can concentrate on refining their strokes and executing efficient maneuvers without the interference of strong current. Moving water and whitewater practices are an opportunity for students to concentrate on judgment and timing in executing maneuvers already practiced.

These elements of a lesson plan offer a controlled setting for students to receive many opportunities to watch demonstrations, practice specific skills or maneuvers, receive individualized feedback and seek additional technical information.

The purpose of an organized progression of activities, where one component builds upon another, is to help paddlers experience a sense of accomplishment and improvement. Stronger direction by the instructor at the outset speeds the introduction and practice of skills. This direction of specific activities also allows the quick spotting and immediate correction of errors. Participants expect constructive criticism in a lesson, and they are looking for guidance in improving their skills.

The organized approach doesn't preclude a relaxed setting. But the time to be more informal in approach is later in the lesson after people have attempted the exercises. More informality is then appropriate as students will have questions about techniques that arise from their practice. At this point, they also need a less organized program that lets them practice at their own pace.

Orientation to Paddling

The orientation provides paddlers with an overview of canoesport and an orientation to basic safety issues. It is usually a dry-land session that prepares students for the activity, and acquaints them with basic strokes.

The orientation acquaints newcomers to the sport with general considerations in paddling.

1. *An Introduction.* The course outline (flatwater, moving water and whitewater) is described as well as what is required of participants. The schedule and organization of the program is explained.

2. *Equipment Review.* Paddlers are acquainted with their responsibility to select equipment appropriate to their skills (boats, paddles, flotation) and equipment that is in good repair.

3. *Clothing Review.* Personal preparedness is addressed (clothing, helmets and personal flotation devices).

4. *Accessory Equipment Review.* Group and rescue gear is reviewed so that paddlers understand from the beginning of their involvement with the sport that groups are collectively responsible for their outings, including accessory equipment.

5. *An Orientation to Safety.* Basic safety considerations are outlined to acquaint participants with inherent hazards in the sport. Their personal assumption of risk should be reviewed, since an instructor cannot guarantee their safety.

Many instructional groups now require that students review an "assumption of risk" form and a waiver of liability before they participate in the activity. The students sign a written statement that says individuals are:

a. aware of inherent hazards in the activity.

b. responsible for judging their own qualifications and safety in choosing to participate.

c. waiving the right to sue instructors and their organization if personal injuries occur during participation.

The review helps to establish that individuals have the ultimate responsibility to decide the nature of their participation in an activity that has inherent risks.

Beyond a general orientation, the introduction is also a time to orient students to more specific technical elements in paddling. Students begin to prepare for a meaningful practice of paddling strokes (explanations and illustrations in *Chapter 7: Strokes*).

- *Basic Biomechanics.* Effective use of the body can create more efficient paddling.

A stretching program can set the stage for introducing strokes. People begin to prepare their inactive muscles for the upcoming program, and various stretches can target specific muscles to be used. Many elements of paddling theory can be delivered as students are stretching their upper and lower bodies. (See *Chapter 5: Conditioning*)

- *Basic Stroke Mechanics.* An understanding of laws of motion helps to relate the execution of strokes to boat reaction.

Participants begin to learn the language of the sport and develop clarity in communication. This stage can be especially important for tandem canoeists who need to understand each other clearly.

One method is the drawing of mock boats in the sand, complete with a center line. Another method is sitting or kneeling in boats on land. Both orient paddlers to basic stroke positions.

A dry-land orientation to strokes develops good habits from the beginning. Instructors provide individualized feedback easily and set the stage for a rewarding on-water practice.

The instructor can walk among the paddlers and use the "hands on" approach to get them and their paddles in the right positions. "Talking" paddlers into position can be confusing, because students can become lost in the words. Instead, move them gently into the correct position, so they know how it feels. The instructor saves time and words and reduces frustration.

The dry-land practice is also important for orienting kayakers and decked canoeists to exiting procedures in the event of a capsize. This "dry" practice of "wet exits" is especially important for participants who are worried about tipping over.

Participants get bored or frustrated with too much dry-land practice, and an instructor must be conscious of the group's desire to get to the water. More technical explanations are often effective when students have wetted their paddles. They will absorb more information when they try the techniques and feel the water against their paddles.

Introduction of Paddling Strokes

The next step is to create a controlled instructional setting to practice strokes. Instructors often use a site at the edge of the pond, lake or river where an appropriate shoreline exists. The water should be deep enough to wet the entire blade and allow a wet exit without hitting the bottom. It should be shallow enough to allow paddlers to empty swamped boats easily.

Canoes can be lined up perpendicular to the shore with the same end (bow or stern) in the water. The setting enables one paddler to learn the stokes, while a tandem partner or another paddler is watching and holding the boat against the shore. The partners take their turn with stroke practice and observation of the other person.

A near-the-shore practice helps students to learn strokes efficiently and to recover easily from capsizes. Some tandem paddlers value the opportunity to learn by watching their partners.

For some, the opportunity to watch other people execute the strokes is an important part of learning; they need a moment to absorb the information before they act. For others, the rest may be necessary before they can continue.

Decked boaters sometimes use a shallow shoreline, where students can place their paddles on the lake or river bottom and practice the dynamics of good boat leans with security.

The near-the-shore setting allows the instructor to walk among the boats if necessary and to help paddlers refine their strokes. It's easier than shouting across an expanse of water to correct problems. If an instructor can eliminate problems near the shore, the subsequent practice of maneuvers will run more smoothly and successfully.

For tandem canoeing, participants should learn to paddle in both the bow and stern positions. Tandem paddlers are most successful when the partners can draw on a shared knowledge of how movement is induced at both ends of the craft. They begin to appreciate each other more fully and to work together as a team. Otherwise, it's tempting to let the other do most of the work, and the boat functions at half-power.

Regardless of any claims that "I'm only a bow paddler," a lesson is the appropriate place for people to experiment with a new position. They can receive the encouragement of an instructor who can give an objective review of their performance. Encourage family members and friends to paddle with new partners. Casting off an old partnership temporarily often allows paddlers to be more adventuresome in trying an unfamiliar position.

The near-the-shore setting encourages paddlers to enter a new paddling world comfortably; they can more swiftly advance from learning a new stroke to executing it properly. That new stroke is now "an old friend" and the paddler will feel more confident about tackling the coming maneuvers.

The three basic categories of strokes are:
1. bracing
2. turning or corrective
3. power

The order in which an instructor introduces the strokes will vary depending upon the abilities of the group and the weather.

In warm weather, beginning with bracing strokes is often effective, because the strokes allow paddlers to become comfortable with balance and boat lean. Balance involves the use of controlled knee and foot pressure and hip flex. An initial emphasis on bracing exercises will encourage passive or timid paddlers to become more aggressive.

Paddlers can brace their paddles on the lake or river bottom to become comfortable with greater boat leans (hip snaps) and more challenging strokes.

The bracing program also deals directly with the fear of tipping over. If people tip over early in the program, then they may be less fearful of the experience. A barrier to learning is reduced or eliminated, and subsequent practice will be less restrained.

Paddlers in closed boats practice wet exits initially to learn boat lean and safe exits from their craft. Open-boat paddlers also need the practice to develop that comfort. After all, whitewater paddlers have to be prepared to swim anything they are paddling in the event of a capsize. The pond is a good, controlled setting for a first capsize.

If poor weather does not allow bracing practice, many instructors begin with turning strokes to foster early success. The boats have a natural tendency to turn, and the paddlers can capitalize on that characteristic by practicing specific turning strokes. Turning strokes also encourage efficient use of the paddler's body.

Power strokes are often introduced later in the lesson after participants have achieved success with turning and bracing strokes. They can be more difficult to learn, and students who have difficulty can become demoralized if they begin with those strokes.

Practice of Paddling Maneuvers

The on-water practice is often blended with the shoreline introduction of strokes to reinforce the effect of specific strokes. Once a series of strokes has been practiced in the controlled shoreline setting, the paddlers should launch their craft to experience fully the effects of the strokes on the boat movements.

For instance, after four or five strokes are introduced at the shoreline, then paddlers can launch the boats to practice maneuvers that use those strokes. Only the immediate practice of specific maneuvers will completely reveal the purpose of each stroke.

Many instructors have used this progression of maneuvers successfully:

1. Bracing — "outrigger" paddle positions for stability.
2. Spins — turning in circles with no forward or reverse motion.
3. Abeams — dynamic lateral movement from a stopped position.
4. Maintaining a straight course forward.
5. Sideslipping or shifts — lateral movement from a moving position.
6. Simulated eddy turns and peelouts — start with forward speed and then turn before hitting the shore; need good practice of No. 4 prior to turns.
7. Maintaining a straight course backwards — good practice for unpremeditated running of rapids in reverse!
8. Rolling — righting a tipped craft without exiting the boat.

Many paddlers need a substantial calm-water practice and suffer in their development when it is cut short. However, other paddlers develop skills quickly and are ready for whitewater almost immediately. As a result, the length of a calm-water practice can vary greatly. Generally, the best experiences in whitewater workshops are often attributed to a foundation established in this initial practice.

If the paddlers are encountering some difficulty, drop back a step. Return to an easier skill introduced earlier, and they can review a familiar move. There's nothing like the appearance of an old friend, in the form of a skill already mastered, to boost the spirits of a new paddler. The practice often helps them succeed in mastering the new move.

Rolling skills are not necessary in the first lesson, because beginners can recover from tipping with wet exits. In addition, the practice of basic stroke skills provides a foundation for rolling practice. A beginner develops paddle sensitivity in stroke practice which is helpful in learning to roll a boat.

However, the ability of new paddlers to develop intermediate and advanced skills is directly related to the ability to roll a craft. The rolling lesson should not be delayed too long, because rolling lessons are an important part of a decked boater's overall education. As early as possible, the paddler must begin to develop the instinctive feeling that the boat is an extension of the body. Once a paddler has mastered basic balance exercises strokes and maneuvers, then it's time to learn to roll. For some paddlers, the appropriate time is the first lesson, but other paddlers may need slightly more time.

Practice Sites with Moving Water

Paddlers need a carefully-planned transition from flatwater to moving river. New paddlers are often tense in their initial exposure to current. They need a practice area in which they can be comfortable in their first attempts at maneuvers in moving water. Successes in such a controlled situation will encourage them to try more difficult moves in faster, more chaotic currents.

Good practice sites enable paddlers to "play the river" and concentrate on refinements of their paddling techniques. The controlled setting allows paddlers to repeat a maneuver until they have perfected it. The practice site also provides an instructor with an opportunity to offer effective criticism and corrective exercises. Information is exchanged in a timely fashion, before paddlers have much of an opportunity to develop bad habits.

Choose a river section which offers a variety of practice sites; the terrain ideally will allow an instructor to build a program of increasing difficulty. Once paddlers become comfortable with basic maneuvers, introduce them to sites which require quicker reflexes, more precise moves and better judgment.

Characteristics of a good practice site include:

1. slow moving water (Class C current) or mild riffles.
2. several eddies along the shorelines and in the river's center.
3. a clear shore (free of scrubby debris or hazards) for rescues.
4. terrain and current that allows students to paddle upriver for repeated attempts.

The current should be strong enough to be mildly pushy so that paddlers can develop a "feel" for its strength and movement. Current that is strong enough to sweep a canoe downriver may be discouraging for some paddlers; the action will occur too quickly for new paddlers to respond without flailing, and they might "freeze" rather than attempt to react.

Fear provides excellent motivation for some people, but most new paddlers do not learn well in an uncomfortable environment. Extreme nervousness undermines their attempts to develop sensitivity for river currents. Choose a location that allows a paddler to, as one instructor says, "keep the butterflies in formation."

A good site may be where an easy rapid ends in a large pool. Bridge abutments create excellent eddies for practice. The confluence of a flatwater river with a whitewater river also provides many options, particularly the ability to review skills in a calm location if paddlers are encountering difficulties in current.

The site should afford good practice of basic maneuvers: upstream and downstream ferries, eddy turns, peelouts and self-rescues. An area relatively free of obstacles allows a paddler to make a mistake and have time to correct the error. A site with too many rocks will not be "forgiving", and a paddler could more easily career into many obstacles. This "pinball" effect can demoralize beginners. Give the paddler an opportunity to develop quicker reactions and better judgment without suffering too much frustration.

Ideal Practice Site

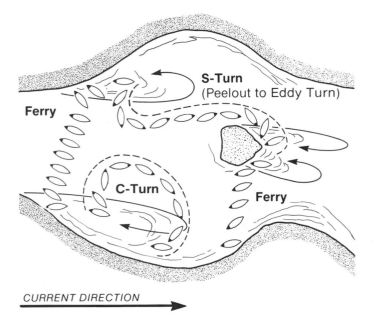

CURRENT DIRECTION

Slow-moving water allows participants to paddle upriver in the shoreline eddies to repeat maneuvers. An instructor can analyze technique in a conversational and, if necessary, "hands on" manner. Partners can rest in the eddy, review their game plan, discuss what went wrong and watch other boats. Instructors can demonstrate efficient strokes and form for maneuvers when paddlers need a reminder. Communication among all is enhanced.

Tandem paddlers can benefit from a practice site by changing positions in the canoes and repeating the maneuvers in their new roles. Encourage paddlers to practice in the bow and the stern so that they understand the responsibilities of each role in a river environment. First-time stern paddlers will appreciate the moving water introduction as they see the river world from a new perspective.

However, paddlers shouldn't remain too long at the first practice site. They may become complacent as the site becomes familiar. The length of stay depends upon the size of the group, the success of the less-skilled paddlers and the opportunities at the site. Ask paddlers to tell you how they feel about their progress and whether they feel ready to move to another site. A fresh start is often the answer to those frustrated paddlers who only need a change of scenery to clear their heads.

A Progression to More Difficult Sites

Next, find a site with slightly faster current. Whether an instructor introduces additional variables, such as more rocky obstacles in the river, depends again upon the group's ability. If paddlers have difficulty in handling the quicker current, then taking them to a rocky rapid will hinder their improvement. They may need more room to move while they learn to react more quickly to the effect of faster current. The choice of a more difficult practice site is an important one.

Faster moving (Class 1) current can provide plenty of action in a controlled setting. Concentrate on peelouts and eddy turns where the current differentials require a solid lean on the boat. Practice eddy hopping so that paddlers learn to control the speed and direction of their ferries. An "S-turn" sequence forces paddlers to change quickly from peelouts to eddy turns.

River running is not overlooked within the multiple practice site approach. In traveling from one site to another, paddlers can learn to dodge rocks effectively. They practice sideslipping to ride the current around the obstacles. Partners learn to work as a team within a tandem canoe.

But the river running practice, while important, adversely affects communication within a group. Instruction may not be as timely as boats practice in a larger area. For the reason, a river trip with multiple practice sites offers opportunities to experience more direct instruction.

Rivers do not always have rapids that build in difficulty. For instance, two good teaching sites may be separated by a rapid too difficult for some paddlers. Every paddler needs to judge whether paddling the rapid is the best course of action. Paddlers must also decide whether other options are more appropriate. These situations offer excellent opportunities within the class to address techniques involved in lining boats along the bank or portaging.

EQUIPMENT

Paddling equipment has changed greatly in recent years, as the aesthetics of natural materials have given way to the function of new synthetic processes. Each has its virtues, but the differences have brought changes in the way that people paddle and have helped to change the character of the sport.

Gone are the days of "all-purpose" equipment, where one basic craft served many purposes. Increasingly, manufacturers are producing specialized equipment for different types of boating as well as individual paddling styles. The diversity of equipment is often overwhelming to a person new to the sport, and an instructor is faced with the task of orienting a newcomer to the differences.

A student will inevitably ask an instructor's assistance in the selection of equipment, clothing and accessory gear. The instructor can advise students about equipment choices, but the decision is ultimately an individual one. Paddlers have a responsibility to select a boat design and equipment suited to their skills, outfit the boat properly and maintain the equipment in good condition.

Personal Clothing

Participants may suffer from exposure to cold weather and cold water if they are not properly protected. The height of the whitewater season is the spring in many regions, but flatwater boaters also need to be prepared for problems that develop from changing weather. The prospect of hypothermia - a severe loss of body heat - is present in every season.

Proper clothing delays the onset of hypothermia, but it doesn't necessarily prevent it. Clothing lengthens the functional survival time of wet boaters, meaning they have more time to get themselves to safety.

"Layering" is a concept that applies to all outdoor sports, and many paddlers use extra layers to increase their warmth and comfort. This system involves the use of:

1. *A wicking layer.* Used closest to the skin, materials like polypropylene or silk transfer moisture from the skin to outer layers.

2. *An absorbing layer.* This middle layer soaks up moisture near the skin and continues to move it away from the body to the outermost layer. Common materials for such garments are wool and new synthetics like pile and bunting.

3. *A protective layer.* The outer layer protects against wind and water. This outer shell is usually made of nylon or laminated materials like Gore-tex® and coated nylon.

For colder conditions, two types of protection are currently popular:

Wetsuits. Constructed of neoprene and often nylon, wetsuits use a layer of water or perspiration next to the skin as an insulating layer. Physical activity heats the thin layer of water, and the neoprene inhibits heat loss to the air. The recommended thickness for paddling is $\frac{1}{8}$ of an inch of neoprene - a flexible layer. Booties are often reinforced on the sole for increased foot protection.

Drysuits. Constructed of a water proof fabric, drysuits are designed to prevent water from entering the suit. Rubber gaskets at the neck, wrists and ankles provide a tight seal; drysuits reduce heat loss as well as keep the paddler dry.

Dampness in drysuits does occur from perspiration or gasket bypass. Use of polypropylene or similiar garmets in conjunction with drysuits is practiced to collect this moisture.

Paddlers must be dressed properly for a harsh environment: cold water, changing weather and river hazards. Well-prepared paddlers use wetsuits or drysuits, personal flotation devices (PFDs) and helmets.

Personal Gear

Personal Flotation Devices (PFDs). Paddlers should choose a U.S. Coast Guard-approved lifevest for adequate buoyancy, physical protection and warmth. Old "horsecollar" kapok models keep only a person's head out of the water, and they do not provide adequate protection or warmth. The "Type III" models commonly used by paddlers feature closed-cell foam in panels around the paddler's upper body. "Type III" PFDs provide high buoyancy, body protection from obstacles and warmth. PFDs need to fit snugly.

Helmets. Closed boaters use a helmet as head protection against injury when rolling their boats. Increasingly, open boaters who are paddling in more difficult rapids with an increased probability of tipping also use helmets. Helmets have a solid plastic or fiberglass shell with a liner that helps to cushion a blow to the head. Paddlers must wear a helmet properly so that the frontal lobe of the head is protected.

Parts of a Canoe

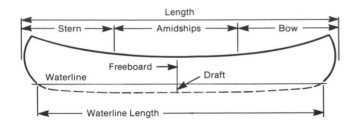

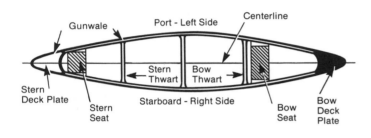

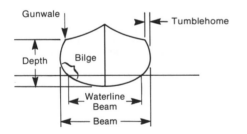

Parts of a Kayak

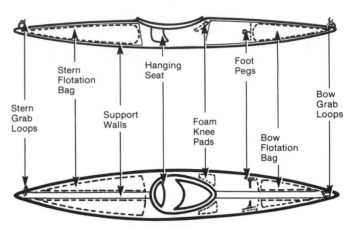

Parts of a Paddle

Canoe

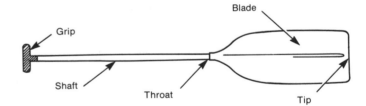

Kayak

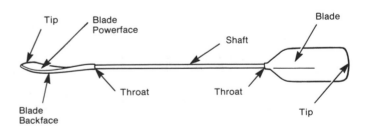

Paddles are constructed of wood, fiberglass, plastic and aluminum. Paddlers' needs will determine their choice of paddles. Higher-performance paddles are lighter and more expensive but sometimes less durable. Paddles used on rugged, remote trips can be heavier and more durable. Aluminum shafts may feel cold to bare hands.

Characteristics of Boats

Boats can have a wide variety of characteristics that effect their performance. The designs are continuing to evolve, primarily as a result of improvements in technology, but the impetus for changes stems from the competitive arena where racers have been seeking lighter, stronger, more functional craft.

Paddlers can now select boats that are geared to their strength, body size and paddling desires. More specialized canoes and kayaks are available to people with specific interests, whether it's racing, touring or playing in the river. Although new technologies have raised the expense of some craft, the improvements in design have increased the *quality* of low-cost boats.

The following diagrams of design characteristics are reprinted by permission of *canoe* magazine:

Length refers to the overall length of the boat from end to end. If the width remains the same, an increase in length will increase the speed and tracking ability of the craft. The length at a canoe's waterline will differ with changes in the stem.

Stem is the shape of the bow or stern along the keel line above water.

Stems

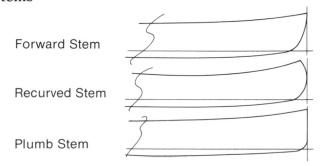

Forward Stem

Recurved Stem

Plumb Stem

Width (beam) of canoes is measured at two points: the molded beam and the waterline. The molded beam width is the distance between the tops of the two sides. The narrower the molded beam width, the easier to paddle because the paddler does not have to reach out as far. The waterline width is the widest point when a boat rests in the water. More weight added to a boat generally will increase its waterline width.

Width of kayaks is measured at the widest point along their length. Whitewater models are widest near the middle, while touring and downriver boats are widest farther back. If a boat widens in the bow and holds the width, it will maneuver relatively easily. If a kayak is narrow in the bow and widens gradually along its length, then straight-line maneuvering is enhanced and turning is inhibited.

Depth in a canoe is measured at the centerline from the gunwale down. A taller boat deflects spray and waves and means a drier boat, but it may catch wind. Shallower depth minimizes wind resistance, but it increases the probability of shipping water.

Depth in a kayak is measured in front of the cockpit. Greater depth means greater room for legs.

Rocker is the shape of the hull along the underwater keel line. The straighter the keel line (as viewed from the side), the more difficult the maneuverability and the easier the tracking ability. If the craft lifts at its ends, then turning is made easier (less drag against the canoe) and tracking harder.

Canoe Rocker

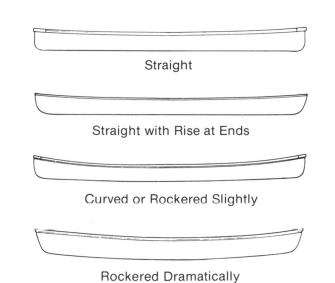

Straight

Straight with Rise at Ends

Curved or Rockered Slightly

Rockered Dramatically

Kayak Rocker

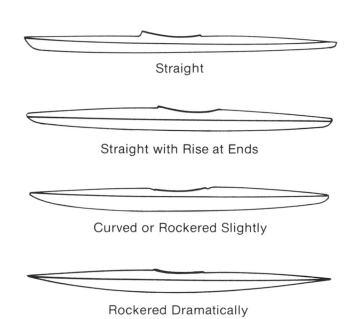

Straight

Straight with Rise at Ends

Curved or Rockered Slightly

Rockered Dramatically

Flare and tumblehome refer to the shape of the boat above the waterline. Canoes with flared sides have greater stability. Canoes with tumblehome have less molded-beam width than waterline width (see "width" above). When a boat with extreme tumblehome is leaned, the stability decreases dramatically.

Flaring in a kayak more often occurs in the bow and prevents waves from rolling onto the boat. The more rounded shape will help the boat lift up over waves. A slalom boat will have flare with a flat deck to reduce the amount of boat that can touch a slalom pole in a race. Tumblehome is generally not a term applicable to kayaks, although it may be found in older sea kayaks.

Canoe Flare and Tumblehome

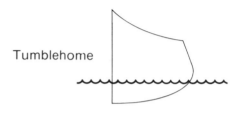

Tumblehome

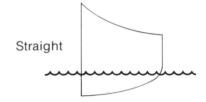

Straight

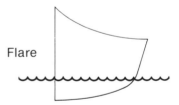

Flare

Kayak Flare

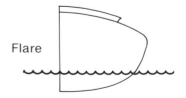

Flare

Symmetry is the shape of the boat from front to back at the waterline, and it affects the boat's efficient movement through the water or its ability to turn. Symmetrical boats (the same overall shape fore and aft) are used for quick maneuvering, such as slalom or playing hard in rivers. Asymmetrical boats usually lengthen and streamline the shape of the bow for more efficient passage through the water. Directional control is increased, while turning ability is decreased.

Canoe Symmetry

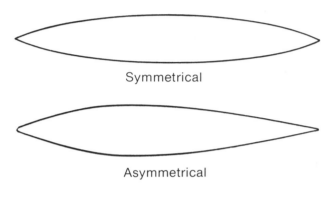

Symmetrical

Asymmetrical

Kayak Symmetry

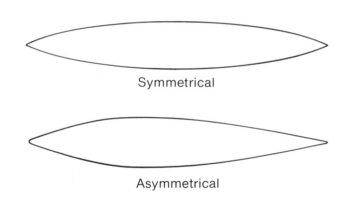

Symmetrical

Asymmetrical

Vees, arches and flat bottoms refer to the shape of the bottom of the craft. Flat-bottomed canoes feel very stable. Very few kayaks are flat-bottomed. More rounded hulls (shallow arch and shallow vee) are initially less stable than flat bottoms, if they have flare but have good stability and are forgiving when the boat is leaned. The greater the vee-shape the better the boat's directional ability, but stability decreases.

Some kayaks have more of a U-shaped bottom with reduced stability (flatwater and, increasingly, wildwater models).

Volume indicates how "full" a boat's shape is or how much weight it can carry. The use of the term has changed in recent years as boats become more low-volume. Higher-performance kayaks and closed canoes have lower volume. Medium-volume boats can carry more gear and are suited for general river running. High-volume boats carry more than 200 pounds and are used for extended travel. The volume of an open canoe is often suitable for carrying hundreds of pounds on overnight trips.

Canoe Vees, Arches, and Flatbottoms

Kayak Vees, Arches, and Flatbottoms

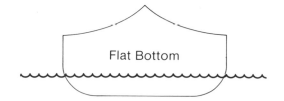

Flat Bottom

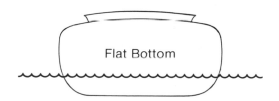

Flat Bottom

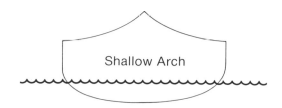

Shallow Arch

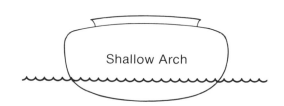

Shallow Arch

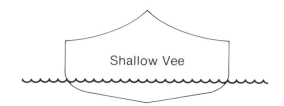

Shallow Vee

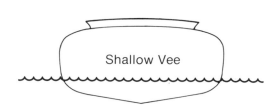

Shallow Vee

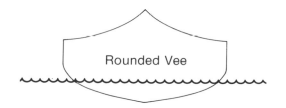

Rounded Vee

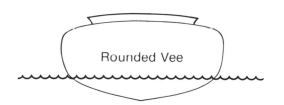

Rounded Vee

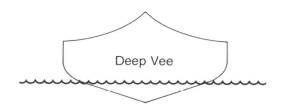

Deep Vee

Deep Vee

Boat Types

The annual *Buyer's Guide* published by *canoe* magazine provides a good look at various types of canoes and kayaks. The following descriptions and diagrams are reprinted by permission of *canoe*.

Tandem Canoes

Casual recreation canoes generally are built of "functional" materials with cost a primary consideration of the consumer. Performance is not a primary consideration, but such things as low maintenance, casual storage and safety are. Boat length will vary.

Day tripper/weekender canoes can carry a weekend's worth of gear and two paddlers. They are lightweight for portability, fairly quick on the water and range about 16 to 17.5 feet long.

Touring canoes commonly are called the traveler's boat. They're long, slender, medium-volume canoes with low profiles. Speed is a primary consideration, and they measure about 17 to 18 feet long.

Wilderness tripping canoes are high volume and can carry sufficient equipment for extended trips into remote areas. They're designed for use under wide-ranging conditions, are high-sided and generally made of nearly indestructible materials. They tend to measure longer than 18 feet.

Downriver canoes are valued primarily for their directional integrity or fast straight-ahead paddling. They have a more sharply-angled stern stem which along with minimal rocker hinders their ability to turn. They're medium-volume canoes with significant depth and are good performers in waters ranging from millponds to open bays to non-technical Class II-III rivers. They tend to measure longer than 17 feet and have higher profiles than touring canoes.

Casual Recreation

Length	16′ 6″
Width	34/33″
Depth	13½″

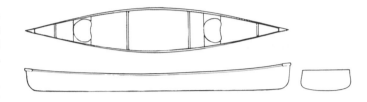

Touring

Length	17′
Width	33/31″
Depth	12½″

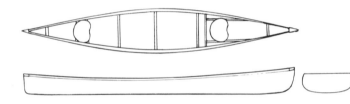

Downriver

Length	16½ to 18½′
Width	32″
Weight	50 to 60 lbs.

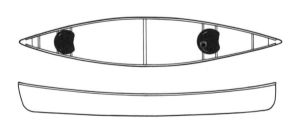

Competition cruising canoes are built to standard length specifications for racing or 18'6" maximum. Maneuverability is not a priority here, but flat-out speed is. They generally are not suitable for normal cruising by anyone other than expert paddlers. They have very low profiles with vertical ends and the gunwales are pinched in at the stern for greater accessibility to the water.

Whitewater playboat canoes usually have a high degree of rocker; they're maneuverable, have high volume and are fairly indestructible with durability having preference over performance. The general range is 16 to 17 feet long; they have full ends to turn away water and float the hull in aerated water.

Whitewater slalom canoes have a high degree of rocker; they're highly maneuverable, have medium volume and can be considered high performance, with performance preferred over durability. They're an expert's canoe and generally have more maneuverability than is manageable for the casual paddler. They average 15 feet in length.

Olympic flatwater tandem canoes are build for straight-ahead speed on calm water. They are 21.3 feet long, 29.5 inches wide, weigh 44 pounds and normally made of mahogany veneer. They are paddled in a high kneel position which requires special instruction and training.

Competition Cruising

Length	18" 6'
Width	32/32"
Depth	11½"

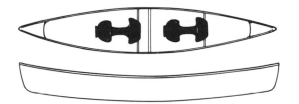

Slalom

Length	at least 15'
Width	34"
Weight	50 to 60 lbs.

Solo Canoes

Cruising canoes are designed with the traveler in mind. Maneuverability takes a back seat to cruising. They're characteristically fast, under 16 feet long with molded beams less than 30 inches.

Racing canoes meet USCA length/width specifications for competition. Maneuverability is not a priority here; speed is paramount. They have very low profiles with vertical ends, and the gunwales are pinched way in at amidships for greater accessibility to the water.

Sport canoes are ideally suited to day-tripping and "just messing around" on a lake or millpond. They balance on a fine line between maneuverability and directional integrity, generally giving initial stability a back seat to secondary stability.

Whitewater canoes (slalom and playboat) are small enough for one person to handle in and out of the water. They're highly maneuverable, generally not beamy (less than 32 inches), with significant depth for volume. They range up to 15 feet.

Olympic flatwater solo canoes are 17 feet long, 29.5 inches wide and weigh 35 pounds. Like the tandem Olympic canoes, they are build for speed, and they are paddled in the high kneel position for maximum power and speed.

Cruising
Length .... 15' 4"
Width .... 22/26"
Depth .... 12½"

Marathon
Length .... 17' 4"
Width .... 31/21"
Depth .... 12"

Sport
Length .... 16' 6"
Width .... 27/24"
Depth .... 11½"

Whitewater
Length .... 12 to 15'
Width .... 25 to 30"
Weight .... 30 to 40 lbs.

Olympic Canoe

	C-1	C-2
Maximum Length	204.72"	255.90"
Minimum Beam	29.53"	29.53"
Minimum Weight	35.28"	44.10"

Kayaks

Casual recreation kayaks are primarily touring boats but will handle nicely in moderate whitewater of Class III or less. They have mild rocker with a cutting bow (or at least narrow enough to penetrate waves and not adversely affect directional stability). They're generally shorter than the average touring kayak or under 15 feet long.

Touring kayaks are very high-volume boats designed to carry generous loads of gear without compromising handling qualities on moderately rough waterways. Most have excellent directional stability, and many have high peaked decks to shed water. They're fairly beamy (25 inches or more) to offer considerable stability and tend to run 16 to 18 feet in length or up to 20 feet for touring doubles.

Sea cruising kayaks are long (often 17 feet or more), high-volume boats designed to cover long stretches of unpredictably rough open water with comparative ease. They're similar to touring kayaks in shape except that many sea boat hulls flare rapidly from a sharp cutting bow to increase lift when penetrating big waves. Others have Eskimo-style upswept ends. Peaked decks add to a dry ride and a low hull profile minimizes windage. Skegs or rudders maximize directional control in crosswinds and currents.

Downriver kayaks are built for straight-ahead speed. They are usually limited by racing specifications to a 15-foot maximum length with a 60-centimeter beam. Most have a radically asymmetrical "Swed" hull form with the boat's widest point well aft of the cockpit. Needle-like cutting bows and vee or rounded-vee bottoms with little or no rocker make downriver boats speedy but hard to maneuver.

Olympic Flatwater kayaks are built for straight ahead speed on calm water. These sleek racing boats are built of wood or fiberglass for singles, tandems and fours. (A strong four man team can pull a waterskier!) Singles are 17 feet long, 20 inches wide and weigh 26.5 pounds. The K-4 is 36 feet long, 23.6 inches wide and weighs 66 pounds; the K-2 is between the single and the four. The cockpit is open allowing for significant leg action for increased power. The boats are quite tippy and often require substantial practice for balance.

Whitewater slalom kayaks are high maneuverable. Some designs have extremely low volume with very sharp edges to keep the deck low and "sneakable" when running gates in competition. These ultralight boats are limited to 13'2" by racing specifications. They're often built so lightly that long-term durability can be a problem.

Whitewater playboat kayaks are medium- to low-volume and built for one use — playing in rapids. They frequently have lots of rocker to aid in quick turns and "hot-dog" stunts. Most have relatively rounded sides to make them forgiving while crossing strong eddy lines or surfing waves and holes. They're available in a wide range of lengths and volumes to match the size of the boat to the size of the paddler. Durability tends to be paramount in their construction; hard play in whitewater can be tough on boats.

Squirt boats are a combination of a whitewater playboat and a slalom boat. They are intended for ease in burying the ends of the craft for "stunt" play.

Whitewater touring kayaks are, above all, high volume so the paddler has plenty of storage space for gear without having to sacrifice too much responsiveness on the river.

Touring

Length	16'
Width	23"
Depth	14'

Downriver

Length	14' 8"
Width	2' 7"
Weight	33 lbs.

Olympic Kayaks	K-1	K-2	K-4
Maximum Length	204.72"	255.90"	433.07"
Minimum Beam	20.08"	21.65"	23.62"
Minimum Weight	26.46"	39.69"	66.15"

Whitewater Playboat

Length	13' 2"
Width	24"
Depth	11"

Decked Canoes

C-1s are closed (covered) canoes for one paddler. These boats are similar in overall appearance to kayaks, although C-1s are generally wider and have a rounder cockpit. C-1 paddlers kneel in the craft and use single-bladed paddles like open boat paddlers. Boat design will vary with usage; downriver C-1s are longer and narrower for tracking, and slalom and play C-1s are shorter and more maneuverable.

C-2s are closed canoes for two paddlers, and they resemble tandem canoes in length and waterline width. Newer models are lower in volume. Cockpit placement can be linear (along an "imaginary" centerline) or offset. Bow paddlers in offset cockpits use a "bow left" or "bow right" position which refers to the side to which the cockpit is offset. Newer slalom designs also place both cockpits close to the boat's pivot point to aid paddlers in negotiating slalom gates.

Slalom OC-1

Length . . . . 13' 1"
Width . . . . 2' 4"
Weight . . . . 20 lbs.

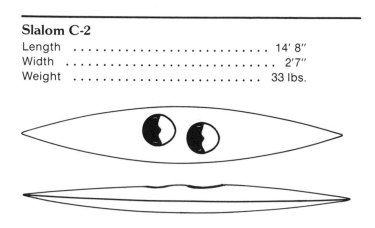

Slalom C-2

Length . . . . 14' 8"
Width . . . . 2'7"
Weight . . . . 33 lbs.

Boat Outfitting

Paddlers must outfit boats safely with a priority on the ability to exit the craft quickly without entrapment or entanglement. Safe outfitting involves several considerations:

Adequate flotation is a necessity for craft so they won't sink when swamped. Closed boat flotation includes inflatable air bags and ethafoam or styrofoam walls that also prevent the deck from collapsing against the hull of the craft. Open boat flotation includes inflatable air bags, styrofoam blocks and inner tubes from tires. The greater the volume of flotation, the greater the displacement of water when the craft is capsized and the easier the boat rescue. Attach flotation securely to the boats.

Thigh straps are used in open and decked canoes to enable the paddler to lean the boat more easily. Paddlers must be able to remove the straps if capsized. Open canoeists using thigh straps are urged to wear helmets.

Spray covers must release reliably. They shouldn't release prematurely under normal boating conditions.

Adequately supported decks prevent the boat from collapsing against a paddler's legs when a decked boat is pinned by water pressure. A person's body should have enough deck clearance to be able to leave the boat in a pinning.

Storage of accessory gear must be secure to avoid a paddler's entanglement with ropes, rope systems and other gear.

First Aid Equipment

Instructional groups often carry first aid equipment for participants in the event of an accident or illness on water or on the shore.

The extent of preparedness depends upon the qualifications of medical personnel in the group — from advanced first-aiders to physicians — and the nature of the trip. Long-distance or wilderness trips require more extensive preparation.

At a minimum, a first-aid kit should contain dressings, ointments, disinfectants, pain medication, emergency phone numbers and health forms for each participant.

Participants with special health considerations (for example, known allergic reactions to insect stings or exercise, diabetes) are wise to carry their medication in the group first aid kit or a personal kit.

Rescue Equipment

Paddlers must carry equipment for unexpected emergencies in their paddling group. Every paddler has a responsibility to bring appropriate equipment.

Throw lines or throw bags are often necessary for rescuing people or boats. Rescue lines and bags are approximately 60 feet long, and throw bags are sometimes preferred to the throw lines because the bags reduce tangling of the rope. Paddlers need to practice with lines to determine their effective throwing distance.

Making a throw bag is easy and inexpensive. The bag is 6" x 12" of medium-weight nylon with a one-inch thick ethafoam disc at one end. The disc helps keep the bag afloat, shapes it for rope storage and helps to anchor the rope without undue stress upon the bag. A drawstring at the other end can be adjusted so that the rope feeds smoothly from the bag.

The rope is usually a 3/8-inch-thick brightly colored polypropylene line that floats.

Throw Bag

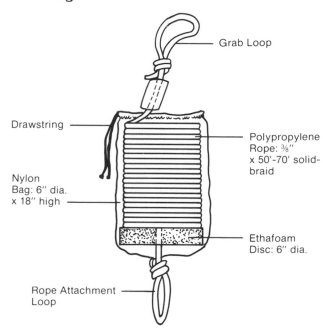

Painter lines on a canoe and **grab loops** on decked boats are helpful in rescues. Painters are easier for a canoeist to grab than loops and allow the paddler to get away from the boat (better visibility and safety).

Accessory gear can include more involved pulley-and-rope systems and repair kits for remote travel.

CONObTIONING

Instructors often field many questions from students about the best ways to get in shape for paddling, because their ability to paddle effectively is directly related to their physical fitness. The nature of a fitness program depends upon the type of paddling, the individual's level of fitness at the outset and the intensity of the person's involvement.

Racers might train to win, recreational paddlers condition themselves to increase their enjoyment, and wilderness travelers may be more interested in increasing endurance for long-distance travel. Paddling can be an incredibly demanding activity in whitewater, or it can be a leisurely, relaxing cruise through a wildlife sanctuary. Regardless of a person's goals, some degree of conditioning will make the experience a rewarding one.

Recreational paddlers can burn an estimated 600 calories an hour when they paddle vigorously. Racers use more calories in a short period of time, depending upon the nature of their efforts, while touring paddlers may burn a similar number of calories over a longer period of time.

As with every physical endeavor, participants experience satisfaction in increasing their body awareness, in developing a sensitivity for essential skills such as balance and rhythm and in stretching the limits of their performance beyond normal exertion. A conditioning program is one way that helps a paddler experience that satisfaction.

This chapter is a primer on conditioning so that new paddlers can begin to understand the relationship between fitness and performance. More comprehensive information is available from U.S. Team publications and specific racing texts listed in the bibiliography.

Components of Conditioning

An individual, whether the goal is racing or recreational enjoyment, must begin by considering four major elements in a conditioning program:

1. strength
2. endurance
3. flexibility
4. cardiovascular fitness

Strength refers to power and speed in the execution of paddling strokes. Increased strength in large torso muscles will increase a paddler's power and speed. Strength is an important consideration for racers or enthusiastic whitewater paddlers who are sprinting or turning quickly across the water.

For developing strength to paddle quickly, the exercises should copy the stroke mechanics as closely as possible.

Recommended Exercises: Short sprints and river playing with lots of "power" moves (enders, surfing); obstacle courses on flatwater that simulate river maneuvers; gates courses in mild current.

Endurance refers to the ability to repeat motions without fatigue. As endurance increases, so does a paddler's ability to paddle for longer periods. Endurance becomes important to long-distance paddlers, whether recreational tourers or down-river racers.

To develop endurance to maintain speed over time, match the exercise rate to the same rate for the event (race, tour, "play" session). The number of strokes should be at least the same number as those used in the event, and the work time should be equal to the target time of the event.

Recommended Exercises: full-length runs against competitors or the clock; daily tours of intermediate and full lengths if preparing for a trip.

Note: Generally, a balanced program between strength and endurance training is recommended: three days per week of endurance training and three days per week of strength training.

Flexibility refers to the stretching ability of muscles or a full range of motion without tension upon the muscles. Stretching strategies are varied (and controversial), but most athletes agree that muscles must be warmed up before stretching is beneficial. Mild activity, such as leisurely paddling or running in place, will warm up muscles.

Stretching prior to intense activity loosens the muscles and "wakes them up" more fully, while stretching after an activity can help to avoid cramping or soreness. Flexibility in paddling directly affects a paddler's ability to rotate his torso into position for strong power strokes and effective turning strokes.

Recommended Exercises: see following illustrations

Cardiovascular fitness refers to the effectiveness of the heart, lungs and blood circulatory system in pumping oxygenated blood to body tissues. Improved cardiovascular fitness means more oxygen in the blood is reaching the tissues which can then work more efficiently. As a result, improved cardiovascular fitness leads to better muscular performance.

Recommended Exercises: see "General Conditioning"

Stretching for Paddling

Shown are stretches that benefit the parts of the body used in paddling. While the sport is sometimes viewed as an "upper body" workout, whitewater paddlers find that their legs are an important factor in leaning and stabilizing a craft.

Publications from the U.S. Team offer more complete information on stretching. The *Trainer Assisted Isometric Stretching (T.A.I.S.)* booklet developed by Frank Novakoski is available from the ACA Bookservice.

Paddlers may find the following stretches helpful in preparing for the sport. The shaded areas in the illustrations show the muscles that should feel the stretch. The arrows indicate the direction in which the body moves. Some stretches can be performed with paddles or with the help of a partner. Remember to breathe deeply and rhythmically when stretching.

Upper Torso, Shoulders and Arms

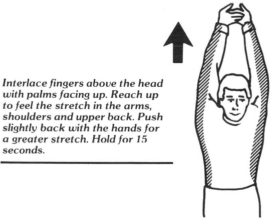

Interlace fingers above the head with palms facing up. Reach up to feel the stretch in the arms, shoulders and upper back. Push slightly back with the hands for a greater stretch. Hold for 15 seconds.

Place palms flat on the ground with fingers pointing to the knees. Lean back slowly to stretch the forearms and wrists. Do not force the stretch. This stretch can relax the grip of students who clench their paddle tightly (along with rotating the wrists in circles). Hold for 20 seconds.

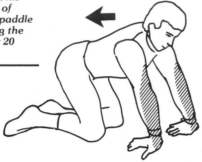

Raise the arms overhead and hold the elbow of one arm with the other hand. Pull the elbow behind the head gently and bend to the side. The stretch is felt from the hips along the side through the shoulder to the upper arm. Repeat for the other side. Hold for 15 seconds.

Hold a piece of clothing or a paddle near the ends with straight arms. Move your arms up, over the head and behind the back. Do not force the stretch. Hold for 10 to 20 seconds.

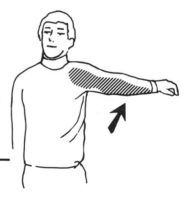

Extend an arm across the chest, reaching out fully. Press the arm against the chest to feel the stretch in the shoulder. Hold above the elbow and pull the arm gently against the chest. Hold for 15 seconds.

Extend an arm fully, level with the shoulder. The stretch occurs in the arm and shoulder. Hold for 15 seconds. Extend the arm rearward at the same level until the stretch is felt in the shoulder. Hold for 15 seconds. Repeat on the other side.

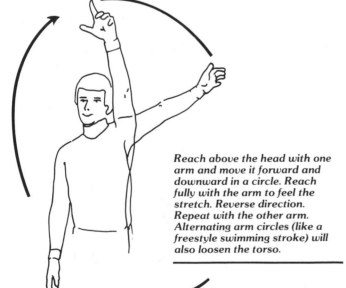

Reach above the head with one arm and move it forward and downward in a circle. Reach fully with the arm to feel the stretch. Reverse direction. Repeat with the other arm. Alternating arm circles (like a freestyle swimming stroke) will also loosen the torso.

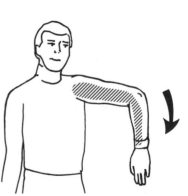

Raise the arm in a 90 degree angle with the palm facing forward (known as external rotation). Rotate the forearm forward and down until the palm is facing backward (known as internal rotation). Extend the rotation until the stretch is felt in the shoulder. Hold for 15 seconds.

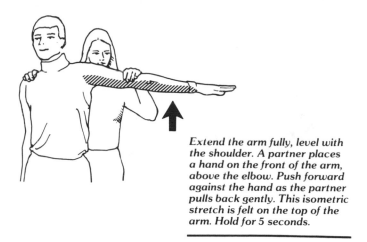

Extend the arm fully, level with the shoulder. A partner places a hand on the front of the arm, above the elbow. Push forward against the hand as the partner pulls back gently. This isometric stretch is felt on the top of the arm. Hold for 5 seconds.

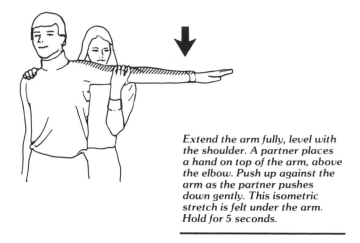

Extend the arm fully, level with the shoulder. A partner places a hand on top of the arm, above the elbow. Push up against the arm as the partner pushes down gently. This isometric stretch is felt under the arm. Hold for 5 seconds.

**Isometric exercises warm the muscles by promoting additional blood flow. They do not build strength.

Lower Back, Hips and Legs

Lie flat on the back and keep the arms straight out at the sides. Lift a leg to a vertical position. Keep the leg straight to feel a greater stretch in the hamstring. Hold for 15 seconds. Alternate legs so that both legs are stretched three times.

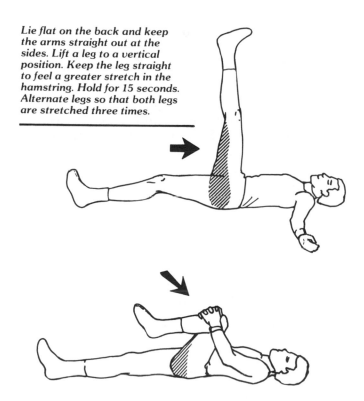

Lie flat on the ground. Lift one knee, grasp it with both hands and pull it toward the opposite shoulder. Hold for 15 seconds to stretch the buttock. Repeat with the other knee.

Lie on your back with bent knees. Keep the lower back and shoulders on the floor. Lift one leg over the other leg. Let the top leg pull the bottom leg toward the floor, until lower back and side of the hip feel the stretch. Hold for 30 seconds and repeat on the other side.

Lie flat on the back with legs outstretched. Lift one knee, grasp it with both hands and pull toward the chest. Keep the head on the ground. Hold for 30 seconds to feel the stretch in the buttock and repeat with the other leg.

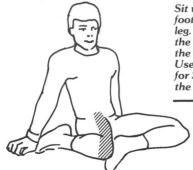

Sit with one leg bent and that foot near the knee of the other leg. Keep the second foot near the body. Slowly lean back until the quadriceps feel the stretch. Use the arms for support. Hold for 30 seconds and repeat on the other side.

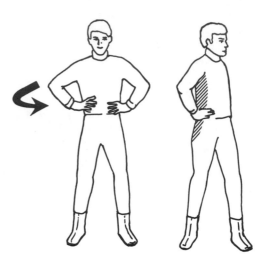

Stand with the feet shoulder-width apart and the hands on the hips. Rotate the upper body slowly to stretch the torso. Hold the position for 15 seconds at the farthest parts of the twist. Hold a paddle near its ends and move it behind the body. Rest it against the shoulders or buttocks for additional stretching.

Keep the feet shoulder-width apart and pointed outward like a duck. Heels remain on the ground, bend the knees and squat down to feel the lower back stretch. Hold onto a tree for support, and hold for 30 seconds.

Sit with one leg straight. Bend the other leg, and cross it over the straight leg with the foot resting outside the straight knee. Rotate the upper body away from the bent knee, supporting the body with one arm and leaning the other against the bent knee. Push against the bent knee to stretch the side and back farther. Hold for 15 seconds and repeat on the other side.

General Considerations in Conditioning

Conditioning is affected by several factors in exercise: its frequency (how often), its duration (length of time), the tempo (speed or intensity of execution) and the type of training (general or specific).

To be effective, exercise should be frequent and of adequate duration and intensity. Sports physiologists recommend these minimums in conditioning activities:

1. three times a week
2. 20-minute sessions
3. a heart rate of 120 beats per minute

The recommended heart rate is a matter of age, weight and physical condition. In determining the appropriate heart rate, the advice of a physician is recommended, especially for participants who are older, heavier and out of shape.

Conditioning occurs in two forms: general and specific.

General conditioning focuses on development of the overall body through a wide range of activities, such as hiking, swimming, jogging, cross country skiing, gymnastics, aerobic dancing, weight lifting and biking. General conditioning offers an excellent way to sense improvements in cardiovascular conditioning. Because poling in cross-country skiing is similar to paddling motions, paddlers are often skiers.

Specific conditioning simulates closely the movements in the sport and strives to develop the same muscles that will be used in the activity. Specific training often provides a feeling of direct accomplishment, because the person is aware of very specific improvements in strength, endurance and flexibility.

While general conditioning is important, physical training that is specific in nature is more important to athletes who wish to excel in a sport. *The best training for paddling is paddling.*

Allow enough time for conditioning to reduce the chance of injury and to increase effective performance. Participants should begin a training program in advance of the paddling season. A full-year commitment to conditioning is necessary among racers, but other participants can modify their involvement.

Paddlers need to match their intensity of training to the intensity of participation early in the season. Individuals who have not prepared themselves for rigorous paddling should not begin the season with an excessive challenge, or injury may result.

Training for Paddling

Instructors face many questions from students who want advice about the best ways to continue paddling after the lesson ends. Students need to remain involved in the sport on a consistent basis in order to further develop their paddling skills.

Paddlers can start with a look at the competitive arena to determine how the successful athletes are training. From training strategies for competition, paddlers can gain an understanding of effective, efficient training programs and apply them for their own purposes.

U.S. Slalom Team Coach William T. Endicott, in his 1980 book *To Win the Worlds*, offers advice to prospective racers that can be helpful in improving paddling performance.

1. *Training in groups.* A highly-motivated group of paddlers keeps each other honest about paddling enough and paddling well. Paddlers can serve as models for each other.

2. *A Supportive Environment.* Performance is affected by emotional well-being, which in turn, is affected by good rest, good food and supportive friends and family who refrain from "constantly telling you what a fool you are to be working so hard on something so frivolous as whitewater canoeing"!

3. *Training in winter.* Large pools or protected stretches of open stillwater keep a paddler active and address the muscles used in paddling (which weightlifting cannot do as specifically). Endicott describes this stage as akin to running with weights on your ankles. The eddy turns are a little harder, because there is no current to help move the boat, but as a result, strength is developed.

4. *Gates on moving water (for slalom).* A moving-water practice site with strong current, a few riffs and good eddies offers an excellent opportunity to develop precision without the fatigue of whitewater rivers. (Instructors are finding increasingly that recreational paddlers develop strong skills through gate sessions.)

5. *Variety in river running and training sites.* New water is mentally stimulating and promotes the development of quick adaptability.

6. *Coaches (or Instructors).* Paddlers need an objective observer for advice on technique and practice strategies. A committed paddler will seek feedback regularly to help improve his performance.

7. *Lots of experience.* There is no substitute for practicing the activity regularly. If racing, one must race a lot to get used to that complex situation. If one wishes to paddle whitewater effectively for recreation, then he or she must paddle a lot to keep skills in consistently smooth form.

STROKES

Chapter VII

A Common Language

The National Instruction Committee, in developing its instructor's manual, seeks to establish an up-to-date reference for technical information in paddling. Strokes at present have many names, and confusion can inhibit clear communication between paddlers. This chapter includes a dictionary of strokes to help instructors remain abreast of changes in terminology.

In an effort to develop consistency in canoesport, the ACA voted in 1983 to adopt the terminology used by the American Red Cross. The two organizations endorsed the development of a uniform language in programs sponsored by both organizations. In this chapter, however, the ACA includes additional strokes that it recognizes beyond the strokes used in Red Cross programs.

The ACA urges instructors to incorporate the changes in terminology in their classes and to support the effort to promote consistency in canoesport.

A New Approach to Strokes

Many similarities, rather than dissimilarities, exist between the strokes for open and closed boats. A number of the same strokes are used by paddlers in all boats, and the execution of the strokes are based on the same principles of motion. However, boat design creates some differences in the execution of the strokes, and paddlers generally modify the "pure" strokes illustrated in the manual as they gain experience in paddling.

This chapter will provide a general overview of paddling strokes for open and decked boats, including a look at paddling theory. Specific illustrations of strokes and maneuvers are addressed in the next chapter.

Types of Strokes

The three basic types of strokes are power, turning and braces.

1. *Power.* These strokes provide primarily forward or reverse momentum.

2. *Turning or Corrective.* These strokes turn the boat so that it veers from a straight course or is brought back onto a straight course.

3. *Braces.* Their primary function is stability for the craft, although they can also help the boat to turn.

The different types of strokes are often combined in a sequence to provide smooth, consistent movement of the craft. While beginners usually practice the strokes in their pure form, experienced paddlers develop combinations of the various strokes. The paddlers' increased sensitivity toward paddle pressure against the water enables them to develop a "feel" for these sequences.

In canoeing, strokes executed on the selected paddling side are called **onside** strokes. Strokes executed on the other side of the canoe are called **cross** (preferred) or **offside** strokes. The canoeists maintain their original grip on the paddle when executing cross strokes.

There are no cross strokes in kayaking, since a kayaker's doubled-bladed paddle eliminates the need to cross over the deck with the paddle.

Strokes can be static or dynamic. A **static** stroke is a fixed-position stroke which requires that the boat be moving faster than the current in order to be effective. The oncoming current strikes the stationary blade, and the resulting deflection of the current forces the boat to move. A **dynamic** stroke is one where the blade is moved actively against the current. The boat can be moving slower or faster than the current.

Parts of the Stroke

The two phases of a stroke are:

1. *Propulsion.* The application of force on the paddle against the water that results in movement of the craft.

2. *Recovery.* The return of the blade to a "catch" position; recoveries can be feathered above the water or sliced under water.

The **catch** or the **plant** is the beginning of the propulsive phase, where the blade is braced against the water in a "ready" position. Paddlers should strive to smoothly blend the phases of a stroke.

Laws of Motion Applied to Paddling

The ability to feel the action of paddling strokes and the corresponding reaction of the craft is the basis of understanding canoesport. A look at how the laws of motion affect paddling can be helpful to a student.

Newton's Third Law of Motion is the primary principle in analyzing physical movement. For every action, there is an equal and opposite reaction. In paddling, the **action** is the application of force on the blade (from the body, to the water). The **reaction** is the movement of the craft in the opposite direction from the force application.

The blade is braced against the water in its strongest position when it is perpendicular to oncoming current (current broached). The blade slips most easily through the water when it is parallel to oncoming current (ie. in recoveries when the paddle is sliced back to the catch). By varying the angle of the blade against the water, the paddler will experience differences in support given by current pressure against the blade. This "feel" is the essence of paddle sensitivity.

Several important principles can affect the movement of the boat:

Trim. The balance of the boat from side to side and front to back. Partners of differing weights can affect trim, as well as unequal distribution of gear.

Pivot point. This point is the balance point of the craft around which the boat is trim — both fore-and-aft and side-to-side. Generally, the pivot point is located near the center of the boat and on the center line. This area provides the most resistance to turn the boat, because it is the point where the boat rests most deeply in the water. (Experienced decked boaters are sinking one end of their boats under water to change the pivot point to that spot.)

Generally, the farther a paddler executes turning strokes away from the pivot point (and its resistance), the more effective the turning action will be.

Ideal Areas for Corrective Stroke Execution

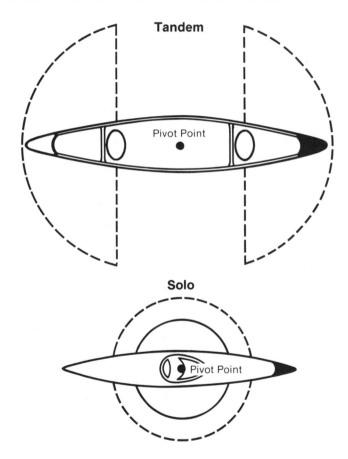

The farther the paddle from the boat's pivot point, the greater the turning ability of the boat.

Rocker. The shape of the hull from bow to stern determines its degree of rocker. The degree to which the ends are curved increases or decreases the rocker; it changes the amount of end resistance against the craft. The greater the rounded ends, the greater the rocker, because resistance to turning is decreased. (See diagram in *Chapter 5: Equipment*)

Boat lean can also affect rocker. If a craft is leaned onto its rounded side or edge, thereby lifting the boat's ends out of the water, end resistance is decreased and rocker is increased.

A boat with increased rocker enables a paddler to execute strokes nearer the body; a boat with limited rocker forces a paddler to reach farther from the boat's pivot point to turn the boat effectively.

Physical resistances. The three types of resistances that affect a craft are: frontal, surface and eddy. A boat can encounter water and wind resistance.

1. *Frontal* resistance occurs where the force of water or wind strikes the craft first. It exerts the greatest pressure against the boat.

2. *Surface* resistance occurs when the water or wind slides along the craft. Smooth boats have less surface resistance than dented boats. Boats with limited freeboard or low volume have less surface resistance than boats with higher sides or volume.

3. *Eddy* resistance is created when the craft displaces water or wind at its widest point. The resulting vacuum is filled in by an unstable whirl of the displaced water. This eddy exerts the least lateral pressure against the boat.

Three Types of Resistances

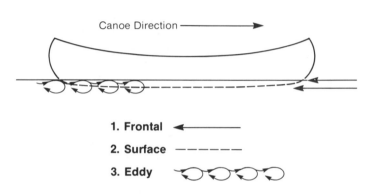

Understanding how physical resistances affect a boat can help a student execute maneuvers more effectively. Corrective strokes are most effective in the eddy-resistance end.

An understanding of resistances helps students to determine which strokes to use in a given situation. For instance, in striving to keep a boat on a straight course, paddlers will be more effective when they use corrective strokes in the eddy-resistance end of the boat. Pressure against the craft is minimized, and the limited pressure enables the craft to shift laterally.

Resistances against the boat will change depending upon several conditions:

1. if the craft is moving forward or backward, then the eddy-resistance end can change from stern to bow.

2. if the craft is moving faster or slower than the currents striking it, then the eddy-resistance end can change from upstream to downstream end.

3. if larger area of the boat is exposed to the currents (wind or water), then the boat will shift more strongly.

A Dictionary of Strokes

This dictionary outlines the various strokes that an ACA instructor can introduce in paddling programs. The ACA does not recommend that an instructor teach all the strokes in every course, since a number of the strokes have similar functions. But the ACA does advise instructors to teach an *adequate* number of strokes for a student to perform maneuvers efficiently.

The characteristics of individuals and their boats affects the type and number of strokes to be offered in a lesson:

- An individual's strength, flexibility, and body size can change the effectiveness of certain strokes. (For instance, good flexibility is helpful in cross strokes. Overweight or out-of-shape students may have difficulty with these strokes.)
- A boat's hull shape can also affect the choice of strokes. (A boat with a high degree of rocker will pivot easily with power strokes, while a boat with less rocker will require more dynamic turning strokes).

In the following dictionary, the side of the blade used to apply the force is not the same for all strokes. The differences are noted by the use of these symbols: powerface (P) and backface (B).

The **powerface** is the side that is pressed against the water during a forward stroke. The **backface** refers to the reverse side of the blade; it is pressed against the water during a back stroke.

Teaching Hint: Paint the powerface of the blade so that the instructor and student have an easy point of reference in analyzing the execution of a stroke.

There is consistency, however, in the use of different faces of the blade. All cross strokes except the cross low brace use the powerface. All compound strokes involve a change from the powerface to the backface (or vice versa) during propulsion.

The dictionary is reprinted with permission of Thomas S. Foster from his third edition of *Recreational Whitewater Canoeing*.

FORWARD POWER STROKES

The strokes are used for propulsion, not correction; the powerface (P) is used in the execution of each stroke.

Tandem Bow Canoe
Forward
Cross Forward

Tandem Stern Canoe
Forward

Solo Canoe
Forward
Cross Forward

Kayaking
Forward

REVERSE POWER STROKES

The strokes are used for propulsion, not correction. Different power faces are listed for the various strokes.

Tandem Bow Canoe
Back (B)
Compound Back (P to B)
Far Back (P)
Cross Back (P)

Tandem Stern Canoe
Back (B)
Compound Back (P to B)
Far Back (P)
Cross Back (P)

Solo Canoe
Back (B)
Compound Back (P to B)
Far Back (P)
Cross Back (P)

Kayaking
Back (B)

ON-SIDE STROKES

These turning strokes move the boat (solo) or the portion of the boat in which the paddler is located (tandem) toward the "on" side of the paddler. For instance, the strokes move the canoe toward port (left), if the canoeist's selected paddling side is port.

All use the powerface (P) unless indicated otherwise.

Tandem Bow Canoe
Draw
*Stationary Draw
Reverse ¼ Sweep (B)
Duffek (Draw-to-Bow)

Tandem Stern Canoe
Draw
*Stationary Draw
Forward ¼ Sweep
Shallow Water Draw

Solo Canoe
Draw
*Stationary Draw
Duffek

Kayaking
Draw
*Stationary Draw
Duffek

OFF-SIDE STROKES

These turning strokes move the boat (solo) or portion of the boat in which the paddler is located (tandem) toward the "off" side of the paddler. These strokes move the canoe away from the paddler's selected paddling side.

The blade face differs for the various strokes.

Tandem Bow Canoe
Pushaway (B)
*Stationary Pry (B)
Pryaway (dynamic) (B)
Forward ¼ Sweep (P)
Cross Draw (P)
*Cross Stationary Draw (P)
Cross Duffek (P)

Tandem Stern Canoe
Pushaway (B)
*Stationary Pry (B)
Pryaway (dynamic) (B)
Reverse ¼ Sweep (B)
**Reverse Duffek (P)
Rudder (P or B)
Shaliow Water Pry (B)
Reverse Sweeping Low Brace (B)

Solo Canoe
Pushaway (B)
*Stationary Pry (B)
Pryaway (dynamic) (B)
Cross Draw (P)
*Cross Stationary Draw (P)
Cross Duffek (P)

Kayaking
Draw
*Stationary Draw
Duffek

STROKES TO MAINTAIN A STRAIGHT COURSE

These turning strokes are used to maintain a straight course forward or backward. They are executed in the "following end" or "eddy-resistance" end of the craft.

The blade face will vary between the strokes.

"Following end" is stern
"J" Stroke (P)
Slice "J" (P)
C Stroke (solo only) (P)
*Ruddering (P or B)
Forward Sweep(s)

"Following end" is bow
Reverse "J" (B)
Reverse "J" modifications (B)
*Ruddering (P or B)
Reverse Sweep(s)

Kayaking
Forward Sweep (P) - if moving forward
Reverse Sweep (B) - if moving backward
Ruddering (B)

BRACING STROKES

These strokes maintain an upright and stable craft. Various faces of the blade are used.

Tandem Bow Canoe
High Brace (P)
Low Brace (B)
Cross High Brace (P)
Cross Low Brace (B)
Turning Braces (high-P and low-B)

Tandem Stern Canoe
High Brace (P)
Low Brace (B)
Cross Low Brace (B)
Turning Braces (high-P and low-B)

Solo Canoe
High Brace (P)
Low Brace (B)
Cross High Brace (P)
Cross Low Brace (B)
Turning Braces (high-P and low-B)

Kayaking
High Brace (P)
Low Brace (B)

*A static stroke which requires that the boat be moving faster than the current to be effective

**A C-2 stroke primarily.

Instructor's Notebook

A Closer Look at Strokes

Understanding how to execute efficient strokes will help students to paddle better. In this section, commonly-used canoeing and kayaking strokes are highlighted to examine their effective execution.

Five special "Instructor Notebooks" offer a closer look at stroke theory, particularly recent changes in paddling technique. These articles discuss effective biomechanics for power and corrective strokes in canoeing and kayaking. Lighter and more conversational in style, these articles were originally published in *The American Canoeist* newsletter to update instructors about technical advances in canoesport. The National Instruction Committee will continue to offer "Notebooks" as a regular feature to instructors. The notebooks provide a forum for addressing paddling issues, discussing trends in paddling instruction and providing further updates on technique.

An Old Friend: The Forward Stroke

The forward stroke in canoeing is a moldy, oldy item. It's been around a long time, like a few thousand years. But this powerful stroke has a new image, and it's time to dust it off.

How do we get people to listen? It's difficult to drop back to basics when paddling students arrive for a lesson and expect to tackle the big water right away.

A whitewater canoeing instructor shared a revealing story about four businessmen from Boston who joined a clinic with their teenaged sons. The fathers had paddled together for several years, and they wanted to introduce their sons to the sport of tandem canoeing on the Androscoggin River.

The instructor prefaced practice of the paddling strokes with an introduction to the concept of torso rotation, where canoeists use the stronger, larger muscles of the upper body to execute strokes. The "torso" style of paddling moves away from the old technique of "arm" paddling. These smaller, weaker muscles produce tiring, inefficient strokes which limit a paddler's power. Within the past five years, videotaped and computer analysis of Olympic paddlers have proven the efficiency of using the upper body's major muscle groups.

"Yeah, yeah," said one father. "Look, I'm not a racer. I'm here to paddle that rapid out there."

Old habits are hard to break, and it can't happen in a weekend, especially when the paddler is calling upon larger muscles, like stomach muscles, which may not have seen this kind of active duty in awhile. But practice of the new technique makes a difference; the muscles begin to respond faster and faster. Instructors need to encourage paddlers to persevere; torso rotation gets much easier with practice.

Effective upper body rotation is helped by paying attention to a paddler's arms. Keep both arms *relatively* straight throughout all phases of the stroke: at the catch (beginning) through the power phase, and during the recovery which is partially under water. (The arms should not be rigid, stiff, or overextended; keep them extended in a flexible, relaxed manner). The straighter arms force a "wind-up" of the upper body, like a coiled spring, which is best seen in the rotation of the paddler's shoulders. The explosion of energy right after the paddle is inserted in the water comes from the uncoiling of the muscles in the upper body. As the muscles uncoil, the force on the paddle is transferred through the body to the canoe. The canoe is propelled forward forcefully.

"I don't know," the father said doubtfully. "It sure feels strange to keep my arms like that. I don't think it's going to do me much good. It's easier the other way."

Meanwhile, the teenaged boys were charging across the practice site and were concentrating on the movements of their upper bodies. The telling moment occurred when the canoeists paddled in the rapids amid the big waves. The boys demonstrated sound technique, solid body mechanics, smooth moves. They executed a higher percentage of their planned maneuvers and watched as the frustration grew in one of the fathers. It's hard to float away from the surfing wave, when other teams are powering into it.

Paddlers need the latest knowledge and skills to move beyond the outdated techniques. The best incentive is watching other paddlers use good torso rotation to execute exciting moves on the river. An instructor who models the correct technique provides wonderful incentive.

The power in torso rotation stems from a few key body positions:

1. The upper body is wound up tightly at the catch position. Why? The result is more explosive "unwinding" and greater power to move the boat forward. Straighter arms force the paddler to insert the paddle farther forward at the catch (remember to keep the angle vertical on the paddle shaft); that farther point makes the upper body wind up more tightly.

2. The hip nearest the paddle may rotate slightly with the upper body as it winds up. But avoid excessive shifting of the hips. Why? The shifting pulls the boat away from the straight forward course. Speed will diminish, because the boat will counterrotate off the course.

3. The torso remains fairly upright; a slight forward bend (15 to 20 degrees) is good, but do not bend backward at the waist. Bending forward excessively drops a paddler's body-weight downward, pushing the boat down before it pops up. Again, the energy goes in the wrong direction, keeping the boat from a straight forward course. The canoe will "plow" or bob through the water.

4. During the power phase, both hands must be away from the body. The paddler must keep a more vertical angle to the paddle shaft (front or "head on" view). The positioning promotes a cleaner power stroke which is parallel to the canoe's center line. As a result, the canoe stays more closely on a straight course.

5. The shoulder nearest the paddle rotates around as the torso winds up like a spring. Why? Good shoulder rotation is a visible sign that the paddler is winding up the torso completely and getting the blade farther forward at the catch. Otherwise, the paddler is bending forward too much at the waist to reach the catch position. (The shoulder farthest from the paddle is the pivot point for the paddler's body; it remains fairly stationary and the body rotates in relation to that shoulder.)

If a paddler doesn't look smooth, or the canoe keeps winding off course, examine the paddler's anatomy for those five points. The most frequent signs are: bent arms, excessive hip shifting, a hunched-over upper body, hands inside the boat and rigid, inactive shoulders.

Help students develop an image of The Perfect Paddler with all the movable parts in the right places. That perfect image, superimposed over a real-life paddler, will help pinpoint the major trouble spots. Focus on those five most frequent errors, and a myriad of other minor problems will disappear.

Power Strokes

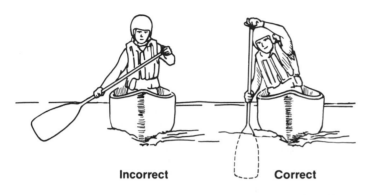

Incorrect   **Correct**

A more vertical angle to the paddle shaft helps to keep an open boat on course. A lower "sweep" position is more likely to turn the boat. Low decks allow a closed boater to modify the vertical position slightly.

Forward Stroke Illustrating Body Rotation

Purpose: To utilize the entire power unit — body and arms — to minimize shoulder dislocations.

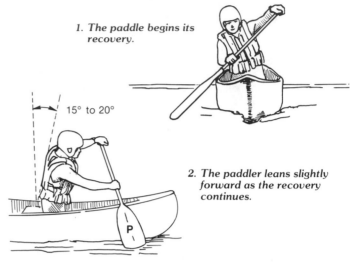

1. The paddle begins its recovery.

15° to 20°

2. The paddler leans slightly forward as the recovery continues.

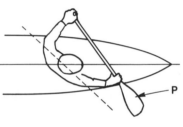

3. The torso rotates to allow a good wind-up before the paddle is planted.

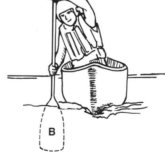

4. The paddle is planted with a more vertical shaft position (70° to water surface).

5. The paddler applies power by unwinding the torso.

6. The stroke ends before the paddle passes behind the body. Note the range of torso rotation through the stroke.

70° to 90°

Recovery phase illustrations 1-3
Force application illustrations 4-6

Short Strokes

A word is needed on the length of the forward stroke, because it's a matter of some debate these days. Where does the power phase of the stroke end? As the paddle passes the thigh, the paddler's body, or behind the body?

It depends upon the situation in which the forward stroke is being used, but the current word is generally to shorten the length of the stroke. When racing or playing hard in the river, a shorter stroke is the most efficient producer of forward power.

Why the shorter stroke? Computer analysis has shown that 75 percent of a stroke's power occurs within the first five to seven inches after the catch. It's the most explosive time, as a paddler's strong torso muscles are unwinding rapidly. That is why racers are forgetting about the longer, languid strokes of yesterday. They are chopping off the trailing end of the old forward stroke, since it provides little power.

Instead, a paddler begins the recovery phase of the stroke before the paddle passes the torso. The top hand (or grip hand) stays high to reduce excessive movement (which results in a loss of time getting back to the catch position). A double benefit results from the new technique. The shorter stroke enables the paddler to capture the most powerful portion and to execute more strokes.

The technique is useful for other whitewater paddlers. The paddler who likes to pursue an intricate river course obtains the same burst of power from the shorter strokes. It enables the canoeist to play in more difficult water or to negotiate through a rocky stretch with fewer touches.

A lake paddler interested in cruising for the day may not need the extra speed afforded by the new technique. But faced with strong headwinds on an unprotected lake, the same paddler needs the shorter strokes for greater power. For more relaxed cruising, the lake paddler can slow the pace or reduce the wind up of the torso. But use of shorter, more efficient strokes will save the canoeist's energy in the long run.

The most persuasive argument for the short forward stroke is that it increases the paddler's "bag of tricks." It provides one more efficient technique which the paddler can call upon when the situation demands it.

The New Improved "J" Stroke

Variations on the basic "J" stroke are plentiful: tripper's "J", slice "J", racing "J". This versatile stroke is often altered to meet many unique situations. Let's examine the modern "J" which is used primarily to maintain a boat's straight course.

The stroke serves the same two purposes as all "J" strokes: it provides the boat with forward momentum *at the same time* that it keeps the craft on a straight course. The two functions must occur simultaneously for the stoke to be most efficient, and it's the simultaneous action which makes the "J" stroke one of the hardest skills to learn.

But the modern "J" goes a step further. It is a variation that enables a paddler to make subtle changes in course, and, often, to increase the boat's momentum substantially. Once a boat veers strongly off course, other "J" strokes and turning strokes are more effective in correcting the course.

Let's review a few basic facts about the "J" before look more closely at its modern form.

First, the initial part of the stroke resembles the forward stroke:

1. Both hands must be away from the body with the paddle shaft more vertical than horizontal (front view). A horizontal angle on the paddle will force it to sweep around, thus turning the boat.

2. Use a rotation of the torso to begin the stroke in a good catch position. Keep both arms relatively straight, but not stiff, to force the torso to wind around and move the paddle farther forward. A coiled body unwinds explosively to give power to the stroke.

Modern "J" Stroke

The "J" stroke begins with a forward stroke (see preceding illustrations). However, move the blade under the boat and carve the "J" by levering the paddle off the boat. Both hands remain in front of the upper body plane.

The first departure from the forward stroke occurs with the positioning of the hands over the water. The top hand on the paddle (called the "control" or "grip" hand) is actually further away from the paddler's body than the lower hand (called the "shaft" hand). With the top hand farther out over the water, the paddle blade is forced under the canoe - closer to the center line or keel of the boat.

Why is that location important? The boat stays on course longer when the blade is closer to the center line and follows that same straight path under the boat. As the blade moves farther away from the center line or keel, the paddle tends to force the craft to turn off course.

The canoeist carves the "J" portion of the stroke by rolling the thumb on the control hand down toward the water. That action enables the paddler to angle the blade into position to brace against the water. (The same power face of the blade is used throughout the entire stroke.) The last push away from the boat should be a quick one, almost a flick of the paddle.

The "J" is carved near the canoe, and the paddler must guard against turning the stroke into a slower, longer reverse sweep. It wastes valuable time and thwarts the stern paddler's efforts to paddle in unison with the bow paddler. Unified paddling provides power that is coordinated; the boat will glide farther as a result. Uncoordinated power results in surging or bouncing through the water which reduces the forward glide.

Beginners are often overwhelmed by the "J" stroke. It's our job to make their learning as easy as possible. Perfecting the "J" takes many miles of practice, and beginners need to know that the problem rests with the stroke's difficult nature, not their own paddling inadequacies!

There isn't much argument with the basics of the stroke. But new variations depart from a pure "J", where no part of the body or paddle can touch the boat at any time.

Certain aspects of the purist approach are absolutely necessary. Keeping one's body from resting on the boat is a wise move. It means the torso is upright and hands are out over the water, where every inch of the paddle must be to execute strokes efficiently.

But improved technology in paddling equipment has brought the sport beyond the days of delicate handling. The loving treatment given birch bark canoes and slim "beaver tail" paddles was necessary to protect the equipment.

The tremendous strides in equipment construction has revolutionized the sport; the equipment can stand up to harder use. The tougher materials in the new products enable paddlers to use their paddles against the boats for greater leverage. Hence, a more aggressive, stronger style of paddling has developed. The equipment is being asked to absorb the impact, not the paddler's body, because the canoes and paddles can take it.

The impact on the "J" stroke is a classic case. Slalom racers and recreational paddlers have discovered the virtues of using the canoe as leverage for a stonger, quicker "J" stroke. When the paddler carves the "J," the paddle shaft is braced against the boat. A powerful leverage off the boat is created, and more dynamic paddling results.

"Impure," shout the purists.

"But effective. And easier," respond supporters of the new style.

In order to use the canoe for leverage, the entire character of the "J" stroke changes. The stroke isn't just stronger; it is also shorter and quicker. The paddler changes the angle on the blade sooner, so the turning portion is a greater and more continuous part of the stroke.

The biggest change is where the stroke occurs: the entire "J" is executed with the control hand in front of the body. The shaft hand will also remain in front of the upper body plane as long as the paddler uses proper torso rotation. The paddle doesn't trail behind the person towards the end of the canoe. The shaft is braced against the boat near the paddler's hips; the blade is slightly aft of this position.

The new position provides the most comfortable place to hold the paddle against the canoe for the best point of leverage. The arms are extended slightly and flexible, where they can pry the paddle shaft off the boat. Avoid the extremes — stiff, overextended arms and cramped arms too close to the body. The paddler will be unable to lever the paddle forcefully.

The positioning also takes advantage of the strongest part of the stroke, just after the catch position. It's a waste of time and energy to continue the stroke significantly behind the body, where the power fades and the best pry position is lost.

Now, who uses the new, improved "J" stroke? Obviously, slalom racers have proven the effectiveness of the stroke with improved times. Recreational whitewater paddlers use the new version to execute more complicated river moves. The quick stroke enables them to exhibit more power and improved fine-tuning in the rapids.

But for those who think the new "J" has no application for "normal" canoeing, consider the advantages for paddlers embarking on overnight trips. Any canoeist who has paddled a loaded boat knows that the leaden weight can wreak havoc with smooth technique and with a paddler's joints. That's where the stress of a heavy craft will appear. If the issue is whether to save a person's joints or save the varnish on the gunwales, choose the body. It's more valuable than the gunwales and harder to replace.

The Other Side Of The Story: Cross Strokes

The former football players powered through the slalom gates in their tandem open canoes with paddles that bent like fly swatters under their strength. Their equipment was less than competitive and their canoes wallowed through the gates. But the finish times were encouraging despite the equipment, and these new competitors were hooked on competition.

That scene occurred in the early days of their program, and those paddlers have made a major change: the exploration of a whole new realm of paddling moves.

Cross strokes.

By definition, a cross stroke occurs whenever canoeists move the paddle from their original paddling side across the boat's centerline to the opposite side of the canoe. The paddler does not switch his grip on the paddle; his hands remain in the same position.

The chief virtue of cross strokes is their efficient, powerful action. Cross strokes don't waste time, and they help to make quick changes in the boat's direction. The seconds which most paddlers save in executing a cross maneuver (instead of changing paddling grips and then switching sides of the canoe) makes a difference in a slalom race.

But the racers aren't the only paddlers who are applauding the cross strokes these days. Recreational canoeists love to catch the difficult waves and surf across the boiling holes. Cross strokes help a paddler dance on water rather than dive to the depths or "blow downstream." It only takes a split second to capsize, and the cross strokes can make the difference between a water ballet or trout scouting.

The strokes come in various forms, and the basis of each stroke is very familiar to all paddlers. One can see it in the names: cross *forward*, cross *draw*, cross *Duffek*, cross *back*.

These principles apply:

1. The cross strokes are used primarily by a tandem bow paddler or solo paddler.

2. The canoeist maintains the same grip on the paddle as in the basic forward stroke. The top hand (called the "control hand") continues its important job of changing the blade angle quickly to execute different strokes.

3. The canoeist uses the same blade face as the one used for the forward stroke (the powerface).

4. The strokes are executed on the canoeist's off side by crossing over the bow with the paddle.

5. The path of the blade is almost a mirror image of the on-side stroke, but the body mechanics have changed.

The cross strokes are initially intimidating stuff for some paddlers. The primary reason is that the strokes demand a flexible upper body, where the torso must twist around to get the paddle into the catch position. Paddlers sometimes feel as if they are twisting around and looking at the stern of their boats.

Most paddlers have to work at developing that necessary flexibility, because they aren't used to the body rotation. Yet with stretching and practice, the cross strokes become easier.

Cross strokes also require that paddlers lean their boats toward the paddle for efficient strokes and stability in current. Balancing on the knee closest to the paddle helps to lean the boat. However, a common problem in learning cross strokes is that canoeists actually lean their *bodies* away from the paddle. They use their bodies as a counter balance because they are hesitant to trust the boat lean.

The counter lean can create problems. C-1 paddlers can catch the upstream edge of their boats and tip. Open canoeists can encounter interference with their strokes. The paddle keeps striking the boat, particularly the gunwale. Proper boat lean tends to lower the gunwale and move it away from the path of the paddle.

Let's examine the **cross forward.** The stroke is executed parallel to the canoe's centerline. Both hands remain over the water, keeping the paddle shaft vertical (front view) to the water. The stroke is short and performed in front of the body. The paddle is returned to the catch position with an underwater recovery when the blade reaches the paddler's knees. (Rotate the control thumb forward, so the blade can slide forward easily.)

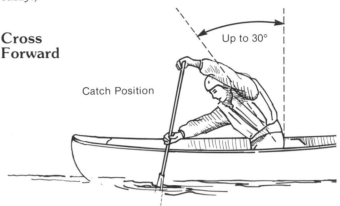

Cross Forward

Up to 30°

Catch Position

1. *The paddle is planted as far forward as a person can lean comfortably, usually up to 30°.*

2. *Paddlers move their upper bodies forcefully to an upright position and stop the stroke at their knees. An underwater recovery helps to establish a quick back-and-forth rhythm.*

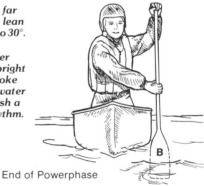

End of Powerphase

Bending from the waist is helpful. The torso may lean forward up to 30 degrees at the catch to help the shaft re-enter the water at a more vertical angle. The upper arm remains relatively straight, while the lower arm and torso rotation or forward and backward body movement applies the force on the power face.

Solo paddlers (OC-1 and C-1) can use a mix of forward and cross forward strokes to maintain a straight course especially starting from a stopped position. For some, the combination may be a good alternative, if they are having difficulty with the J-stroke.

Execute a ferry by using a cross forward on the downstream side of the boat. It can help to promote solid and stable boat lean in rough water.

Tandem bow paddlers often use the cross forward in combination with turning strokes to execute off-side eddy turns and peelouts. It allows a smooth transition from turning action to power to stay in eddies or to continue downriver.

The **cross back** is more often used by solo paddlers, and it requires good upper-body flexibility. Paddlers cross over the boat with the paddle and insert the blade opposite their hips. Because the powerface is used, paddlers must rotate their bodies until their shoulders are almost parallel to the boat's centerline. The stroke is executed parallel to the centerline and ends near the knees.

The cross back is a powerful way to stop a boat quickly to scout a rapid, and it is usually used with a back stroke to maintain position in the river.

Cross Back

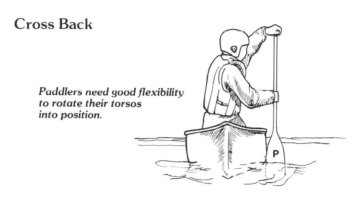

Paddlers need good flexibility to rotate their torsos into position.

Two turning strokes — the **cross draw** and the **cross Duffek** — are very similar, but they do have important differences. Both strokes pull the bow toward the paddle powerfully. The torso rotates to allow the paddle to reach the catch position, and the body unwinds to supply the power to bring the canoe to the paddle.

The **cross draw** is planted in the water about 60 degrees from the canoe's centerline. The stroke is executed with a more horizontal angle on the paddle shaft. The control hand stays relatively low — at the armpit or lower. The "control hand" arm is flexed while the shaft arm is relatively straight. A cross draw using torso rotation is a powerful stroke. By comparison, a cross draw performed only with the arms provides less power.

The **cross Duffek,** also known as a "cross turning high brace," resembles the cross draw in its basic action, but the paddle shaft is held more vertically. The control hand is held higher which enables the canoeist to brace the paddle against the current. The high hand position permits a more efficient and smoother transfer to the cross forward. The cross Duffek combines bracing with turning action; the paddler gets greater stability from the brace.

The cross Duffek is initially a static stroke which uses the force of the current to turn the canoe; paddlers develop "a feel" for the moment when the bracing support of the cross Duffek ends, and a dynamic stroke is needed to continue the turning of the canoe. The stroke usually flows into a cross forward stroke.

The cross Duffek provides great stability in performing peelouts and eddy turns. It helps to provide proper boat lean for the maneuvers. The paddler is able to lean solidly into the turn, particularly when strong currents in the river demand a solid downstream lean. After an off-side eddy turn, a cross forward can help to prevent the canoe from sliding out of the eddy.

The **cross forward sweep** is the stroke most likely to make paddlers feel as if they are tied in knots. It is used by decked boaters more than open boaters, since it isn't as effective as other strokes in moving a heavier boat. The cross forward sweep is a mirror image of a forward sweep. While its major disadvantage is the awkward position on the cross side, it can be very effective. If a paddler is already on the cross side of the canoe, one or two cross sweeps can change the course of the boat very quickly and provide the initial torque for an onside turn (OC-1, C-1).

Exercises for Cross Strokes:

Stretching. Exercises that simulate the paddling strokes are a good place to begin. Use a broomstick or a paddle across the shoulders and twist slowly from side to side to mimic the torso rotation. Hold the tightly-coiled position for 10 to 15 seconds. Increase the rotations gradually as your flexibility develops. Try alternate toe touches, and work up to 200 touches. Then hold five- and 10-pound weights and work up to 100 touches.

Circle drills. On flatwater and in current. Using only cross strokes, leave an eddy (offside peelout), turn in the current and return to the same eddy (offside eddy turn) without removing the paddle from the water. Use under water recoveries to increase stability.

Ferries. Using a cross forward on the downstream side of the boat, leave an eddy and ferry across a river stretch into another eddy. The exercise orients a paddler to good boat lean. Change the boat lean as you enter the eddy.

In general, mild current with a safe run-off is a good place to begin practicing cross strokes. A good practice site with several eddies allows students to refine their control in executing eddy turns, peelouts and ferries. They won't mind experimenting — stretching the extra couple of inches and risking a tip. That's when the real improvements occur, when paddlers test their limits and find that they can go farther than they think. Boats aren't tippy; canoeists are!

Moving Ahead with Kayaking Strokes

Beginners often arrive in a kayaking lesson with a shopping list of skills to learn — from strokes to maneuvers to rolling a kayak. It's difficult to meet every goal, especially in shorter lessons, but an exploration of fundamental skills can help.

Crucial to a beginner's development is an awareness of boat lean and basic body positions in executing strokes. Developing a "feel" for good body mechanics will establish good paddling habits from the beginning.

A common scene is the beginner who interprets boat lean as "body lean" and extends the body over the water in executing strokes. Resting weight on the paddle is a dodgy proposition at best, since the paddle gives limited support. Beginners who "overlean" in this fashion tend to swim a lot, or they spend time recovering wildly from one move to the next.

An early orientation to effective boat lean establishes a good foundation for subsequent stroke practice. Beginners will feel more secure within their boats once they have discovered the range of balance allowed by the boats.

Boat lean is effected by pulling up with one knee and simultaneously pushing downward with the opposite hip. The move involves an active shifting of weight downward through the hip and an ability to balance on that hip. Through the weight transfer, paddlers move the boat under them and roll the boat on its side. A paddler's body weight remains above the boat throughout the move.

A related skill is a smooth shifting of weight from hip to hip. Paddlers can practice alternating the "knee-pull hip-push" action to experience the transition. They can experiment with "C" positions; the high sides of their bodies will be crimped in "C's" as they balance on each opposite hip. The low side is stretched. This crimping action is part of a crisp hip snap so important to many kayaking moves.

Incorrect boat lean

Correct boat lean

A well-fitting boat helps a beginner to feel more secure with these moves. Paddlers need three points of solid contact against the boat to be able to balance the craft: a snugly-fitting seat, knees pressing against the deck and balls of the feet pressing against the foot braces.

Basic **body positioning** involves more than a paddler's weight over the boat. Envision the paddlers who are slumping in their seat. The design of some seats encourages paddlers to slouch on their tailbones rather than sit more upright on their buttocks. Leaning backwards in this slouched position prohibits kayakers from using their bodies powerfully to paddle. Sitting upright allows the upper body a greater range of motion.

That's important in kayaking strokes, because the ability to rotate the upper body through a stroke increases the stroke's power. The larger, stronger trunk muscles are propelling the paddle more strongly through the water. The smaller, weaker arm muscles generally give less thrust and tire more quickly.

Kayaking strokes involve a "push-pull" action against the paddle. Paddlers punch out with their upper arms as they pull back with the lower arms. It's the boxing approach to kayaking, and boxers get better punches when their big, upper bodies follow the punching arm.

Rotating the body also serves another important function. It forces paddlers to keep their trunk and shoulders facing their hands. Keeping the hands in front of the plane of the upper body reduces the chances of shoulder dislocations from the arms moving behind and away from the body.

Let's examine several power strokes in terms of these fundamental skills.

The **forward** stroke is most effective when using good body mechanics. Paddlers punch out with the upper arm between shoulder and eye level. The shoulder swings around to obtain a good forward reach at the catch position, and that action forces the torso muscles to rotate and wind up. The more tension on coiled muscles, the greater the force (power) in the release of tension.

After the blade is inserted next to the boat, the arm pulls back until the hand reaches the hip. The corresponding rotation of the torso actually winds it up on the opposite side in preparation for the next stroke. The other hand should not cross over the centerline of the boat, although it blocks out a clear view of the bow. The paddle blade is removed from the water by lifting the wrist and elbow to shoulder level as quickly as possible. This action promotes a clean exit and a quick recovery to the next stroke.

Common inefficiencies with the forward stroke are a failure to submerge the blade fully, leaning forward or hinging from the waist (rather than torso rotation), crossing over the centerline with the upper hand, making the stroke too long, and failing to pull the paddle parallel to the centerline and near the boat.

Beginners need time to practice forward strokes because the boats will turn naturally (as they're designed to do). Keeping the boat on a straight course requires a feel for timing and power that may be elusive initially.

The **back** stroke retraces the forward stroke with the same body mechanics. The catch position is just behind the hip, and the power phase ends when the upper hand is near the shoulder. Beginners should look backward over *one* shoulder. Their tendency is to turn the stroke into more of a sweep or bend from the waist during the stroke.

Forward Stroke

1. *Torso is rotated with right shoulder forward; upper hand passes closely by the ear, lower arm nearly straight.*

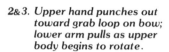

2&3. *Upper hand punches out toward grab loop on bow; lower arm pulls as upper body begins to rotate.*

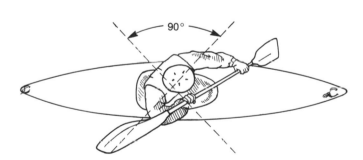

4. *Upper hand punches to full extension of arm and upper body follows through to full rotation.*

5. *Paddler prepares for next "catch" on other side (left). Note torso is rotated now with left shoulder forward.*

Back Stroke

1. *Torso is rotated with left shoulder back; upper hand is in front of head with arm slightly bent 90°.*

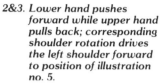

2&3. *Lower hand pushes forward while upper hand pulls back; corresponding shoulder rotation drives the left shoulder forward to position of illustration no. 5.*

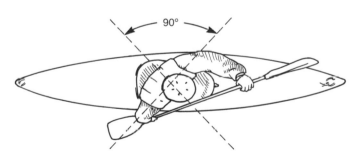

4. *End of powerphase of back stroke; note shoulder rotation.*

5. *Paddler prepares for next "catch" on other side (right). Now the right shoulder is back.*

The **forward sweep** is a beginner's best friend. When all else fails (especially the forward stroke), the sweep is often the answer. The stroke turns the boat as well as moves it forward, and it's invaluable in getting a kayak back on course without losing too much momentum.

Paddlers begin the stroke near the bow and move the paddle away from the boat in an arc toward the stern. The most important part of the stroke is the arc of the blade opposite a paddler's body. Paddlers should be extending the paddle fully at this point to get away from the boat's pivot point. The farther the paddle from the pivot point, the more effective the turn.

An effective sweep employs good boat lean. They maintain a fairly upright body position (toward the sky not toward the water), while the boat leans into the stroke. Beginners usually feel comfortable with only minimal boat lean, until they develop confidence with recovering from that lean and shifting their weight to a neutral position over the boat. Aggressive forward sweeps involve a paddler's experimentation with that "point of no return" from courageous boat leans.

A forward sweep also uses a "push-pull" action. The arms are comfortably straight (the lower arms straighter than the upper arm), and the body is wound up at the catch. The body unwinds as the paddle is pulled out and around in the arc. Paddlers sometimes envision their shoulders parallel to the paddle shaft, and the shoulders face the shaft in this position throughout the stroke movement.

Common inefficiencies are a failure to submerge the blade fully, leaning or hinging the body forward (rather than torso rotation), arching the body backward (rather than torso rotation), reaching down rather than out on the arc, holding the hands too high (keep them low enough to reach out farther) and leaning with the body not the boat. Some beginners will actually lean away from the stroke to counter balance the paddle (as if they are moving away from something distasteful!)

If paddlers appear rigid with little rotation through the stroke, the introduction of the back sweep may help them to loosen up.

The **back sweep** retraces the path of the forward sweep and involves the same considerations for boat lean and body position. Increased body rotation can be effected by beginners turning around and looking at where the blade is inserted. They are more likely to move their head and shoulders in order to get a less unobstructed view of paddle if it's in the right position.

The hands are held lower on a back sweep with the paddler's knuckles skimming over the sprayskirt. Watch beginners for a tendency to bend forward from the waist when the paddle is at the catch.

Teaching Exercises. After students become acquainted with the basic stroke mechanics, they can experiment with moving the kayaks in a straight line. Obstacle courses provide variety in what can become frustrating practice. Arrange markers to achieve different objectives: triangular courses for straight running and turning on one side; "giant slalom" style markers (offset greatly) for gradual changes in direction; "slalom" style (offset slightly or not at all) for quick changes in direction.

Variations on a Theme: the Draw Stroke

When a paddler starts talking about the "draw" stroke, an appropriate question might be: "Which draw?" One paddling pundit's favorite answer, especially in whitewater, is "a quick draw."

The "draw" in kayaking seems to have endless variations that are modifications of the basic stroke. A "pure" draw is performed at a right angle to the paddler's side, where the person reaches out with the blade, inserts it fully in the water and pulls the boat to the blade.

Both hands are extended over the water, and the paddle shaft remains at a vertical angle through the stroke. Most of the force application toward the boat is from the lower hand. The stroke ends with the blade near the boat when the paddler still has room to slice the blade backward for a recovery above the water. Paddlers should strive for an underwater recovery where the blade slices back to the catch position.

The paddle blade is inserted parallel to the centerline. The draw will move the boat sideways, generally with little turning action, when the entire boat is in flatwater. It's a good stroke to help paddlers change their position and shift sideways in an eddy.

Then the variations begin. They are an effective means of orienting beginners to the "feel" of their paddle blade against the water. They are valuable training exercises to help paddlers move from the draw stroke to a more committing stroke like the Duffek. The variations require subtler changes in the paddle position at the catch and in the angle of the blade against the water.

Beginners can experiment with putting an angle on the blade by cocking their wrists backward. That action "opens" the blade so that it is exposed to oncoming current (the powerface of the blade faces the bow). The more exposed the to oncoming water, the greater the turning action.

Lowering the top hand will change the paddle shaft to a more diagonal angle (rather than vertical). This action moves the paddle into a high brace position — the position of security for beginners in negotiating rapids. Slapping the paddle gently against the water in this position helps beginners to feel the support that the blade can offer.

Another variation is changing the position of the paddle. Paddlers can move the blade from opposite the hip to in front of the knee, still reaching out comfortably as far as possible. The blade (with the powerface toward the body) is pulled diagonally towards the body, and stopped just behind the knee. The action moves the boat forward as well as sideways, and it can help to position the kayak in the right channel for negotiating rock gardens.

Still another variation is possible from that catch position in front of the knee. By cocking the wrists backward, paddlers turn the powerface toward the bow. They can then move the blade toward the bow just as canoeists do with a draw-to-the-bow stroke. Underwater recoveries allow paddlers to execute repeated draw strokes and to experience more dynamic turns. It is often used to position a kayak for exiting eddy with a peelout. This exercise again establishes a foundation for the Duffek.

The "low" High Brace.

Kayak paddlers often use a "low" high brace, especially when entering the fast main current from an eddy. The brace is placed with the shaft at right angles to the boat about eight inches in front of the paddler. The paddler reaches out as far as possible and places the powerface on the current. The edge of the blade nearest the bow should be slightly elevated (a climbing angle) to prevent the blade from diving and to allow a "low" sweep to the bow for a more crisp turn.

Talented beginners are ready for the Duffek when they have practiced good boat leans and good "low" high braces. They are developing a feeling for good balance, and just as importantly, they are discovering the point at which body weight has to return to a neutral position to maintain good balance (the "point of no return"!)

The Duffek requires an orientation to several additional points:

1. The paddle blade is always in front of or to the side of the body.

2. The upper arm position is low; the forearm moves to the forehead so that the arm frames the face. (The upper arm can also be across the chin or neck.)

These positions keep the body "tighter" and the action forward of the body rather than extended with the blade behind the body. The latter position can invite possible shoulder dislocations.

Additional fine tuning is needed to reach the Duffek position:

1. The paddle shaft is almost vertical to the water surface, usually around an 80 degree angle to the water surface.

2. From the forward stroke position, the wrists are cocked backward to open the powerface of the blade to oncoming current.

3. The blade is "opened" until it broaches this current.

4. The upper arm is across the forehead with the hand over the opposite shoulder; the lower arm is bent, relaxed and extended slightly forward and over the water at a 45-80 degree angle from the centerline of the boat.

5. Proper positioning of a Duffek can be checked by the paddler's ability to easily see the stern of the boat.

The Duffek is usually held for several seconds as a brace or "anchor" around which the kayak will turn, and then it is drawn toward the bow. The stroke is converted smoothly to a forward stroke to continue moving the boat toward its destination. This finishing of the turn also requires that paddlers modify their strong boat lean to a more neutral posture. Timing is crucial; this more complex move requires that paddlers combine several variables at the right moment.

Common inefficiencies include leaning the body, using a lower-position brace rather than a higher-position Duffek, keeping the upper arm away from or above the forehead and extending the lower arm too much (rather than leaning the boat) and too stiffly, planting the paddle behind the body.

Paddlers with a clenched grip can try a variation with their upper hand; they can hold the paddle with a thumb and finger to promote a more relaxed grip.

The Duffek Stroke

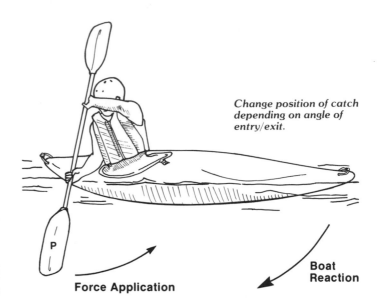

Change position of catch depending on angle of entry/exit.

Boat Reaction

Force Application

Kayak paddlers (and canoeists), after having mastered proper boat leans when entering or leaving eddys, often learn to execute a Duffek stroke. This stroke is used in the "entering" current to make the turn faster. The paddler's shoulders should be rotated so the upper body faces the blade upon insertion. All Duffek strokes use the powerface and the insertion is always in front of the paddler (45° to 80° from the bow centerline). The stroke does not provide a beginner (or any paddler) with the bracing support of a "low" high brace.

Technique Analysis of Strokes

The positive approach is best: there are no errors, only inefficiencies! Execution of a specific stroke is not necessarily "wrong," particularly if it gets the job done, but it may be inefficient. Beginners will respond better to an instructor's analysis of "inefficient" rather than "bad" or "incorrect" technique.

In addition to being demoralizing, a preoccupation with "correct" style also can be misleading. There are too many instances of athletes demonstrating a technique contrary to an accepted style, yet they win their competitive events. While general guidelines exist for efficient execution of specific techniques, the final form depends greatly upon individual characteristics such as body type, strength and endurance.

A Place to Begin

Technique or movement analysis begins with a look at the relationship between a paddler's body and the paddle and their effect upon the craft. Superimposition of "an efficient paddler" over a student can help an instructor analyze the action and spot deviations from efficient form.

Two basic approaches are used in movement analysis:

1. a cause-symptom approach
2. an symptom-cause approach

The first approach involves an initial look at the paddler's torso to analyze his or her basic body position. Common inefficiencies include a forward lean caused by "hinging" from the waist, a backward lean creating an arch in the back and inadequate rotation of the torso. Any of these causes will affect the arms, and by extension, the action of the paddle against the water. Bent arms usually means the upper torso isn't moving fully, and strokes will be less powerful.

The second approach reverses the process and starts with the symptoms such as boat performance and the path of the paddle. Trace the problem back through the hands and arms to the torso to find its cause. Common inefficiencies can include the boat bobbing or "porpoising" through the water (dipping the paddle too deeply and dropping the body), boat rocking or "wallow" from side to side (excessive weight shifting from the knees or hips), lack of boat lean (no weight shifting), lack of extension with the paddle (hands inside the boat) and paddle skipping (paddle too shallowly in the water, shaft angle and body position may need changing).

Additional causes of inefficient technique can be related to equipment: improper paddle size, seat height or fit, a craft unsuitable for type of water, a craft unsuitable for paddler's abilities.

A Positive Approach

Feedback is an integral part of the learning process, and students look to an instructor for help in evaluating their progress. Evaluations must be positive, clear and concise.

A positive approach to critical analysis involves three steps: initial praise for some aspect of the performance, a specific suggestion to improve an inefficient action and encouragement to incorporate the new information.

The best approach is correcting only one inefficiency at a time, because people are generally unable to concentrate effectively upon many new variables at one time.

Remember: praise is always appropriate!

Videotape Analysis

The adage "a picture is worth a thousand words" is especially true in technique analysis of physical skills. As with other sports, paddlers have discovered the benefits of videotaping students to help them improve skills quickly.

Videotaping enables new paddlers to correlate what they are "seeing" with what they are "feeling". The visual image can be slowed or stopped to show inefficient technique, and it can be used as a basis for recommending changes in body or paddling mechanics.

Videotaping is most effective when paddlers can view themselves at least twice. Practice of the recommended changes and subsequent taping enables students to witness their accomplishments and reinforce their learning.

MANEUVERS

This chapter addresses paddling maneuvers for each craft and illustrates specific strokes that can be used to execute the maneuvers. The maneuvers include:

1. spins
2. forward straight
3. reverse straight
4. sideslips or shifts
5. eddy turns and peelouts
6. bracing
7. ferries
8. rolling

Various combinations of strokes are illustrated for each maneuver to show the many ways that paddlers can perform a given move. The choice of strokes often depends upon a paddler's comfort with particular strokes and the nature of the body of water. Some strokes will work more efficiently in flatwater (ie. pushaway), while others will be more appropriate for current (ie. Duffeks).

The maneuvers for canoeing are divided into "on-side" and "off-side" moves rather than "left" or "right" maneuvers. The intent is to enhance communication between paddlers and the instructor in introducing the maneuvers and to help tandem paddlers communicate more effectively on the river.

The point of reference is the selected paddling side of the tandem bow paddler or solo canoeist (the side of the boat where they execute forward strokes). For instance, an on-side eddy turn or peelout means that a boat is turning toward the tandem bow or solo canoeist's paddling side. An "offside" eddy turn or peelout refers to a canoe turn away from the paddlers' selected side.

For students who have difficulty knowing "left" and "right" directions, the change in terminology gives them a clear point of reference. Also, on-side (or off-side) skills required to perform a maneuver remain the same when a paddler switches paddling sides. This is not so if "left" or "right" adjectives are used.

Introduction to Tandem Canoeing (OC-2, C-2) Maneuvers

Tandem canoeing is a cooperative venture, and the challenge in the sport is more than just learning the maneuvers. Working well with a partner is an integral part of successful tandem paddling. Effective communication between partners is essential, and the strong team is one where partners understand their roles in each end of the canoe and work together to paddle the boat. An even stronger team is one where both paddlers have experience as a sternperson and bowperson.

Paddlers need to understand:

1. the complementary bow and stern strokes that, when used together, form the basis of all maneuvers.
2. the reaction of each end of the craft when a specific stroke is executed.
3. the reaction of the craft as a whole when a stroke is used.

Neither paddler should switch sides indiscriminately. Each person should paddle on a side opposite his or her partner to balance the craft. Paddling on opposite sides helps to equalize the power of the paddlers and permits them to use paddles as braces (like training wheels on a bicycle).

Paddlers in the "following" end of the canoe, most often the sternperson, have a responsibility to:

1. follow the proper general course in the river, ie. river center, left or right, by choosing a route with the other paddler.
2. maintain the craft's alignment parallel to the current (this is easiest if done in the "following" or "eddy-resistance" end of the canoe) or change the alignment to set up a particular move.
3. maintain adequate spacing relative to other craft.
4. assist upstream canoes by pointing at the proper course.
5. relay messages up or down river.

Paddlers in the "leading" end of the canoe, most often the bow, have a responsibility to:

1. read the immediate route in the river.
2. decide the appropriate strategies and maneuvers and communicate these decisions to their partner.
3. take immediate action to execute the strategy for negotiating the river in anticipation that partners will follow their lead.

Initially, most communication between partners is verbal, but non-verbal communication develops as individuals gain experience together. Experienced tandem paddlers can play extensively on a rapid with little talking; they simply react to each other's strokes in relation to the river environment.

Instructors can encourage students to communicate with their partners about maneuvers or route choices as opposed to strokes. For instance, if one paddler tells another person to "draw," the paddler may not understand why the stroke is necessary. The "stroke calling" method encourages one paddler to rely blindly upon another person in the operation of the boat. While it may be helpful in specific situations that require quick action, it shouldn't be developed as a habit.

The better approach is communicating a desired maneuver such as an "offside" eddy turn or a direction such as a "sideslip away from the ledge." Then both paddlers understand where they want to move the boat, and they can contribute equally to that movement.

Canoeists who claim that "I'm only a bow paddler" should be encouraged to experience the stern position during a lesson. Support and feedback from an instructor can be helpful in reducing apprehension about the stern role.

Paddle selection is an important consideration for tandem paddlers. An efficient paddle size is one that matches a person's upper body. When the blade is submerged fully during a forward stroke, the paddle grip should be around eye level. A paddle that is too long will often force a paddler to execute sweep strokes that can send the boat off course.

Introduction to Solo Canoeing (OC-1, C-1) Maneuvers

The solo paddler in an open canoe (OC-1) or decked canoe (C-1) is the bowperson and sternperson combined. The following general guidelines apply:

1. When the paddle is ahead of the pivot point, the paddler functions like a bowperson (see preceding section for bow responsibilities).
2. When the paddle is behind the pivot point, the canoeist functions like a sternperson (see preceding section for stern responsibilities).

Whether a solo paddler functions like a bow or stern paddler depends upon whether the boat is moving faster or slower than the current. The same laws of motion apply to the solo craft; turning strokes are most effective in the eddy-resistance end of the craft.

When learning to execute eddy turns and peelouts, a beginner sometimes finds that stern strokes feel more secure, particularly low braces. But using tandem bow strokes will lead to quicker, crisper turns.

Solo canoeists (OC-1) sometimes find that it helps to gain experience tandem canoeing in the bow and stern. The ability to control a tandem craft is an invaluable experience for easing the transition to solo paddling.

The solo paddler should kneel slightly aft of the center of the craft, since the force necessary to turn the craft is most efficient when it is applied as far as possible away from the pivot point. At this location, the canoeist can obtain maximum extension fore and aft of the pivot point.

A beginning solo canoeist should select a paddle which is two or three inches longer than the length normally used for tandem stern. For most individuals, the paddle length ranges from 56 to 62 inches.

Solo paddlers should not switch paddling sides indiscriminately, and they should learn to maintain the same control-hand and shaft-hand positions for all the strokes, including cross strokes. An accomplished solo canoeist can paddle well on both sides of the boat without changing the original grip.

Introduction to Kayaking (K-1) Maneuvers

Like decked canoeists, kayakers use light, responsive boats to move quickly across the water. Kayakers sit in their craft and use a double-bladed paddle with feathered blades to execute strokes. The feathered blades, offset from each other by 75 to 90 degrees, enable the blades to be returned to the catch position in an automatic feathered position to reduce wind resistance.

Paddles can be flat-bladed or spoon-shaped with one side of specific paddle control. A "right-hand" or "left-hand" control indicates that the designated hand maintains a firm grasp on the paddle and controls the angle of the blades. The other hand permits the shaft to rotate within the grasp between strokes but holds the paddle firmly during the stroke.

Most paddlers uses a right-hand control paddle, because they are the type most commonly sold; whether a person is left-handed or right-handed does not make a significant difference. Beginners do need to practice cocking the wrists fully to rotate the blade into the correct position to grab the water.

A kayaker can determine the type of hand control by examining the powerface of the blade. If a kayaker takes a power stroke on the right side of the craft and the powerface of the opposite blade is facing up, then he has a "right-hand" control paddle.

A beginner slalom paddler chooses a paddle that ranges in length from 198 to 210 centimeters.

Kayakers grip the paddle in the palm of their hands rather than the fingers. The palm grip, closer to the wrist, makes it easier to cock the wrists and gives a paddler better control over the paddle. Beginners sometimes hold the paddle with their fingers and may find the paddle snatched away by current.

Kayakers grip the paddle in such a manner so that, during a forward stroke, the upper hand is no higher than the head while the lower hand may skim the water. If a paddler holds the paddle above his or her head, proper hand positioning on the paddle is generally greater than shoulder width at a point where the elbows are at 90-degree angles to the forearms (and the forearms are at 70 to 90 degrees to the paddle shaft).

An extreme shift of hand position — closer or farther apart — will jeopardize the ability to execute efficient strokes and to stabilize the craft with solid braces.

Teaching Hint: Tape the proper grip location on the paddle when a beginner shifts the grip repeatedly.

Paddling Maneuvers

The following explanations of maneuvers are reprinted by permission of Thomas S. Foster from his third edition of *Recreational Whitewater Canoeing*.

Stroke Illustration Explanations

Key

| — Single line indicates a static or fixed position stroke which requires that the boat be moving faster than the current (static strokes marked by asterisk)

|||||| — Indicates a dynamic stroke with a tip-first water entry; shaft comfortably verticle to water surface

|||||| — Indicates a dynamic stroke with an angular entry of the blade (usually between 30° to 70°)

|||||| — Indicates a dynamic stroke with a horizontal entry of the blade; shaft comfortably low to water surface

(B) — Use backface of the blade to apply force

(P) — Use powerface of the blade to apply force

- - - - → — Indicates action of water against paddle and resulting angle of deflection

——→ — Small arrows of strokes show direction of force application

——➤ — Long arrows indicate reaction of boat and direction of boat movement

▶ — Darkened end indicates bow of boat

Note: Kayak illustrations use a right hand control paddle.

Sample Illustration

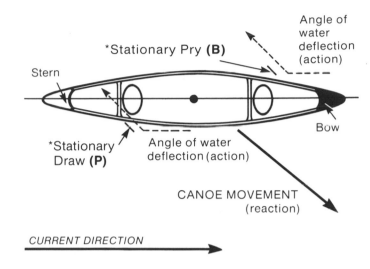

*Static or fixed position strokes which require that the canoe be moving faster than the current to be effective.

Maneuver: Spins

Spins turn the craft with little forward or astern movement; turning on a point, called the pivot point, which is generally at the amidship of the craft. (The "stern pivots" used by more advanced paddlers are not addressed here.)

Tandem (OC-2, C-2)

Draw - A paddle stroke designed to move the craft to the "onside" of the paddler or toward the powerface of the blade. The force application is against the powerface with both hands over the water; the shaft is vertical.

Pushaway - A stroke designed to move the portion of the boat in which the paddler is located toward the "offside" of the paddler. The force application is against the backface with both hands over the water; the shaft is fairly vertical. This stroke is used primarily in flatwater maneuvers and seldom in the river, because there are more powerful, efficient strokes that accomplish the same result.

Sweeps - Wide, shallow strokes used for turning a boat. The shaft is held low, and force is exerted on the powerface (forward sweep) or backface (reverse sweep). This action creates an arc as far away from the craft as possible. Sweeps are executed as 90-degree arcs in tandem paddling or commonly as 180-degree arcs in solo paddling. A cross forward sweep used in solo paddling also applies force on the powerface.

Duffek - A dynamic stroke by a tandem bow or solo paddler that uses the powerface of the blade for a force application toward the bow. Used mainly to enter an eddy in an "eddy turn" or leave an eddy in a "peelout." To use it, the paddler places the forearm on the forehead with the control thumb down, inserts the blade in the water 45-80 degrees from the bow and then draws toward the bow. The angle of insertion should permit the powerface to current broach the current being entered. This stroke is a dynamic one, but it may not appear so because of initial frontal resistance on the blade. As the boat slows, the bow will turn to the blade.

Cross Duffek - Same as Duffek but executed on the "offside" of the paddler's designated paddling side. The respective positions of the control hand and shaft hand on the paddle remain unchanged. The paddler rotates the shoulders so the chest faces diagonally offside, places the blade in the water 45-80 degrees from the bow and then applies force toward the bow. Use the powerface with the control thumb turned away (out).

Reverse Duffek - This tandem stern stroke is sometimes used in close cockpit C-2 turns, especially for eddy turns and peelouts. It uses the powerface for force and is similar to a reverse sweep in location, but the shaft is fairly vertical. The forearm is on the forehead; body rotation is essential.

Spins

Onside

Offside

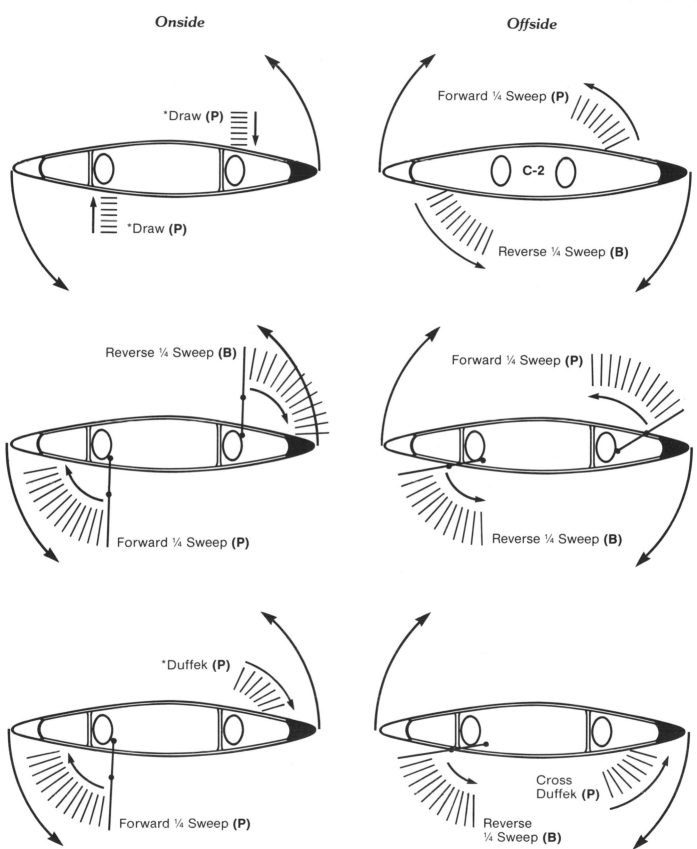

*Note: Underwater recovery; turn control thumb out.

Spins

Compound Reverse Sweep - This stroke is a combination of the reverse quarter sweep (see sweeps) and the Duffek. Paddler rotates the shoulders, places the blade behind the body near the craft and holds the shaft as horizontal as possible as a force is applied in an arc. When the blade reaches a right angle to the boat, the paddler flips the control thumb down and continues a force toward the bow with the forearm on or near the forehead.

270-degree Sweep - A combination of a cross draw (90 degrees) and a forward half sweep (180 degrees). The powerface is used for force application. Paddlers should maximize shoulder rotation; recovery is above the water. The leading edge on the recovery is the edge nearest the sky during the propulsive phase.

Onside

Offside

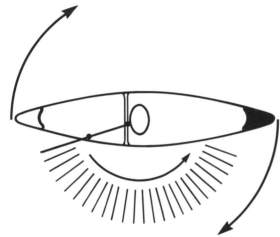

Reverse ½ Sweep **(B)**

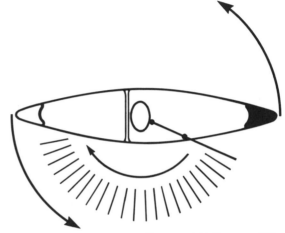

Forward ½ Sweep **(P)**

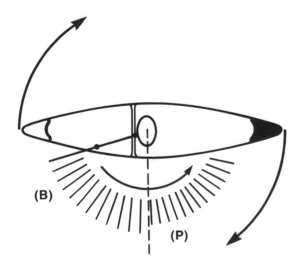

Compound Reverse Sweep

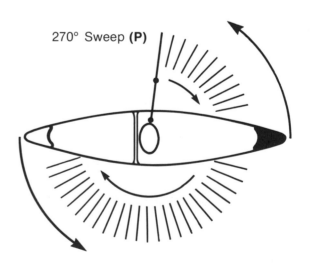

Spins

Forward Sweep - The stroke turns the bow to the offside of the stroke. The blade is inserted near the bow (by winding up the torso) and sweeps around in a wide arc toward the stern by unwinding the torso. The end of the stroke is critical. To make it more effective, keep your eyes on the blade and bend your back arm. The most important part of the stroke is the arc as far away from the body as possible at a position opposite the pivot point. The paddler's body remains upright and relaxed, and the knees are used to lean the kayak toward the blade (press the knee farthest away from the blade against the deck).

Reverse Sweep - The stroke turns the boat and moves it backward. The blade is inserted near the stern (by rotating the torso backwards) and sweeps around in a wide arc toward the bow (by unwinding the torso and rewinding it forwards). The same rules apply as outlined above, while the hands are held slightly lower, just over the cockpit.

Onside

Offside

Forward Sweep **(P)**

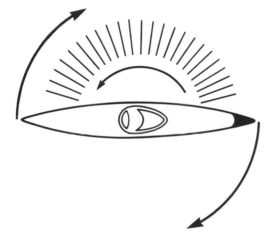

Reverse Sweep **(B)**

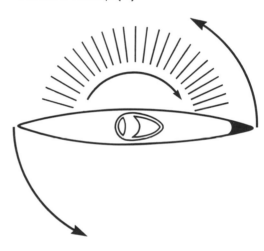

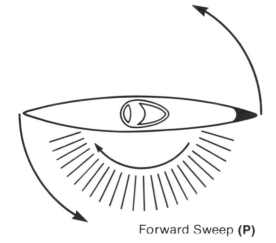

Forward Sweep **(P)**

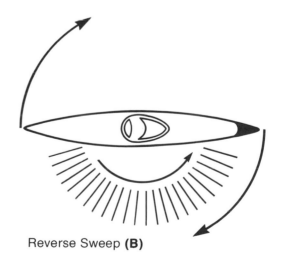

Reverse Sweep **(B)**

Maneuver: Forward Straight

Tandem (OC-2, C-2)

Forward - See complete description in *Chapter 7: Strokes.*

Standard "J" Stroke - Begin with a forward stroke. When the blade is under the canoe near the knee, roll the control thumb away toward the bow. As soon as the control thumb is rolled, begin moving the blade out from under the boat in a diagonal direction away from the canoe and behind the paddler. Keep rolling the control thumb down toward the water and continue to push water away from the canoe as the blade continues back and diagonally away. The stroke is completed when the blade is at a right angle to the water surface and the arms have reached maximum extension behind the body.

In a "pure J", neither the paddler's hand nor the paddle touch the canoe during any part of the stroke. Both hands are over the water during the propulsive phase.

Any "J" stroke or modification is used by the person in the "following end" when the canoe begins to veer off course to this person's off paddling side. The amount of force executed by a given "J" depends upon such variables as wind, current, craft speed and the degree to which the boat is off course.

Modern "J" - A shorter version of the standard "J." Begin with a forward stroke. When the blade reaches the paddler's knees, abruptly roll the control thumb away toward the bow and then pull the paddle grip (control hand) toward the paddler's off-side. This results in a dynamic pry of the shaft off the gunwale or side of the boat. The contact point between shaft and craft is adjacent to the paddler's side; *the paddle blade is slightly aft of the paddler's buttocks.* Recovery is immediate and partially under water at the outset. Most of the recovery is above water, however, and fairly close to the boat if the control hand is held high.

The entire stroke is executed with both hands in front of the body, which deviates from the standard "J" in its positioning.

See complete description in *Chapter 7: Strokes.*

Solo (OC-1, C-1)

"C" Stroke (P) - Used to get the boat underway without veering off course immediately. The "C" is a sequence of strokes: a draw to the bow, a forward stroke and a "J" stroke. It is more effective if the "C" is executed well under the craft during the forward stroke.

"J" Stroke (P) - See above.

Cross Forward (P) - A forward power stroke used in getting underway as a subsitute for the "J" stroke. Paddlers cross over the bow and insert the blade in the water with a 30 degree forward body lean. Keeping the upper arm straight, the paddler applies force by moving back with the body and pulling hard on the shaft hand. Recovery is under water by turning the control-hand thumb away and keeping the upper arm straight. The propulsive phase stops when the blade reaches the paddler's knee.

Tandem (OC-2, C-2)

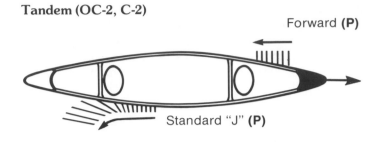

Forward **(P)**

Standard "J" **(P)**

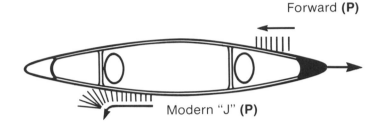

Forward **(P)**

Modern "J" **(P)**

Solo (OC-1, C-1)

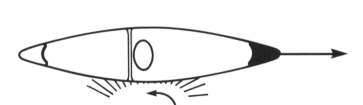

"C" Stroke **(P)**

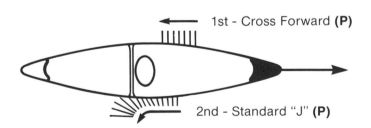

1st - Cross Forward **(P)**

2nd - Standard "J" **(P)**

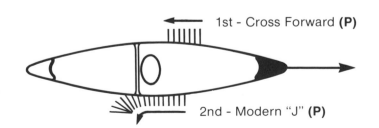

1st - Cross Forward **(P)**

2nd - Modern "J" **(P)**

Kayaking (K-1)

Forward - Moves the boat forward. The kayaker pulls the paddle with the lower arm and shoulder, while the upper arm and shoulder push the paddle through the stroke. The motion is similar to a boxer's punch, where the upper hand is pushed out at eye level. The upper hand does not cross over the centerline on the deck during the propulsize phase of the stroke. Reach with a straight lower arm to insert the blade as close to the bow as possible, and the stroke ends when this pulling hand reaches the body.

The paddle blade is removed from the water by lifting the wrist and elbow to shoulder level as quickly as possible. This process results in a clean exit and a quick recovery to the next stroke.

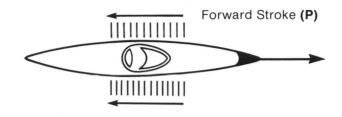

Forward Stroke **(P)**

Maneuver: Reverse Straight

Tandem (OC-2, C-2)

Reverse Standard "J" - A reverse of the standard "J," the stroke is executed by the bowperson (in the "following end" of the canoe) and uses the backface of the blade. Slice the blade into the "catch" position just aft of the body and execute a back stroke. As the blade passes the body, turn the control thumb down toward the side of the craft and continue to apply force diagonally away from the body.

Reverse Modern "J" - Using the backface, begin with a back stroke. When the blade is at the knees, abruptly turn the control thumb down so the blade is almost at a right angle to the surface and then dynamically pull the control hand to the offside of the boat. Pry off the backface of the paddle with the shaft and the craft in contact near the paddler's knees.

Solo (OC-1)

"J" Strokes - See above.

Crossback - Cross over the boat with the paddle and insert the blade opposite the hip, using the powerface for the force application. Apply power parallel to the boat's centerline and stop just beyond the knees. Recover underwater by rolling the control thumb away from the body and slicing through the water to the catch position.

Farback - Rotate the upper body toward the stern and insert the paddle as far back as possible to obtain at least a 70-degree insertion to the water surface. Using the powerface, apply power toward the body. Recover underwater by rolling the control thumb away from the body and slicing through the water to the catch position. The closer a paddler reaches to the stern, the more the boat will move backwards in a straight line. Modify the farback by inserting the blade farther from the stern (within a 45-degree angle from the boat's centerline). The boat will then move backwards and toward the paddle. (See illustration next page)

Compound Back - A combination of a farback and a back stroke. Use the powerface during the farback, and change to the backface as the paddle moves past the hip to finish with the back stroke.

Tandem (OC-2, C-2)

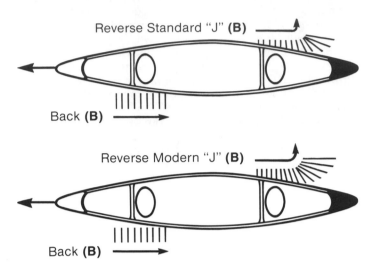

Solo (OC-1, C-1)

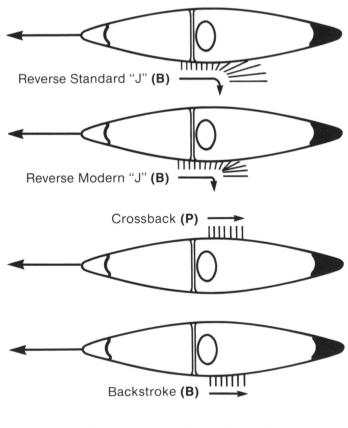

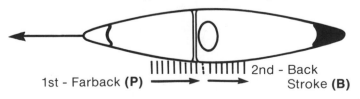

Solo Canoeing (OC-1, C1)

The Farback Stroke

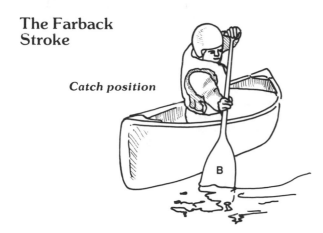

Catch position

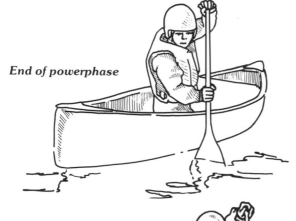

End of powerphase

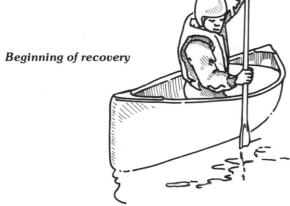

Beginning of recovery

End of recovery

Kayaking (K-1)

Back - Moves the boat backward. The stroke begins just behind the hip and moves toward the bow with the blade as close to the boat as possible. The paddler pushes with the lower arm and pulls with the upper arm for power. The stroke ends when the upper arm nears the eye and the blade is as close to the bow as possible (without leaning the body forward). The shaft is held quite vertical with the upper hand crossed over the centerline through the first half of the power phase.

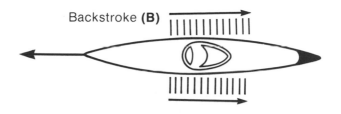

Backstroke **(B)**

Maneuvers: Sideslips (Shifts)

These maneuvers are used to avoid rocks when paddling downstream — either forward or reverse. They shift the boat sideways and generally keep the boat in alignment with the current. The strokes may be executed in either a static or dynamic manner. An initally static stroke often needs more force, and therefore, is converted to the complementary dynamic stroke.

Sideslips are used most commonly in open canoes; decked boat paddlers generally turn, paddle forward and then re-align with the current to avoid an obstacle. In any case, sideslipping is done well in advance of oncoming obstacles; otherwise, use the decked boater's strategy.

Tandem Paddling (OC-2, C-2)

Stationary Draw - A static stroke with the powerface deflecting oncoming water (frontal resistance) at an angle, causing the craft to move both toward the paddle and parallel to the blade. Both hands are over the water; the shaft is vertical or near vertical and held adjacent to the body (tandem) or aft of the body (solo). A sculling action or a diagonal draw will allow the paddler to maintain the angle and convert to a dynamic action.

Stationary Pry and Pryaway - A static stroke with the backface deflecting oncoming water at an angle, causing the craft to move in a direction parallel to the blade and away from the paddler's designated side (offside). The paddle blade is under the bilge and the frontal resistance literally forces (jams)

the blade against the canoe. The shaft is near vertical and can be converted to a dynamic action by pulling the control hand hard toward the body. Start with the blade well under the bilge and use short strokes (12″) with an underwater recovery.

Shallow Water Draw - The stern stroke is simply the last half of a forward ¼ sweep (see sweeps), but the forward momentum has been almost eliminated. Most of the action draws the stern sideways.

Shallow Water Pry - This powerful stern stroke uses the craft as a fulcrum to move the boat away from the blade. The shaft is low, and the blade is inserted in a fairly horizontal manner. If it seems difficult to pry off the boat, a reverse sweep is a great tandem substitute as it will not only force the stern to the offside, but it will slow the craft's downriver speed.

Cross Draw - A tandem bow or solo stroke used to move the canoe or part of the canoe to the paddler's offside. The canoeist's hands do not change position on the paddle. The paddle is crossed over the boat and placed fairly horizontally in the water to draw water with the powerface. The torso rotates to allow the paddler to reach the catch position, and the body unwinds to supply the power to bring the bow of the canoe to the paddle.

*These static strokes require that the craft be moving faster than the current (creates frontal resistance in bow). This is usually the case unless the paddler(s) has been arresting downstream movement by back paddling which causes the bow to experience eddy resistance.

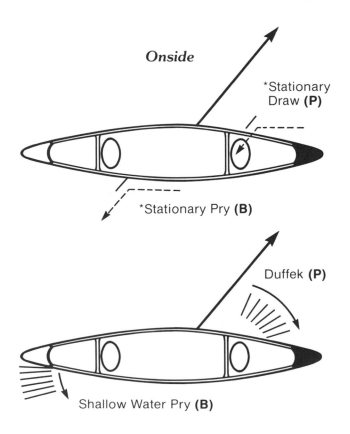

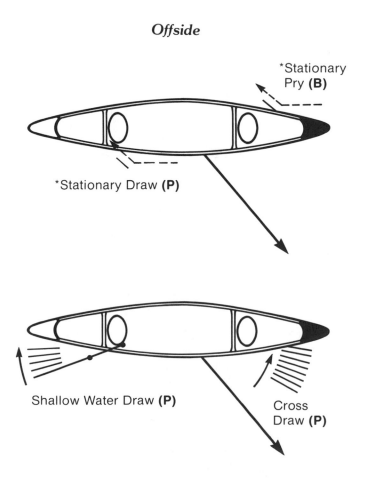

Note: These static strokes require that the craft be moving faster than the current.

Solo Canoeing (OC-1, C-1)

Stationary Draw - See description above.

Cross Stationary Draw - Same as the stationary draw except executed as a cross stroke. Paddler rotates torso to allow paddle entry into the water just aft of the body.

Pry Strokes - The pry strokes are more commonly used by open canoeists. C-1 paddlers risk capsizing their craft when prying, because the dynamic action pushes the boat edge under water.

Onside

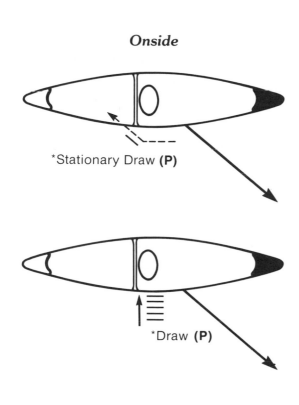

*Stationary Draw (P)

*Draw (P)

Offside

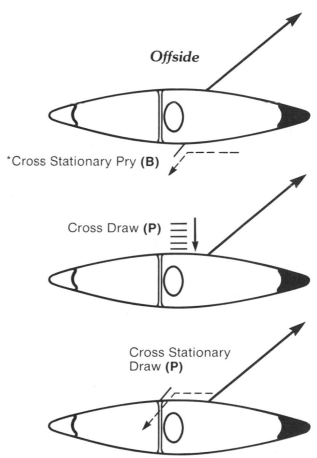

*Cross Stationary Pry (B)

Cross Draw (P)

Cross Stationary Draw (P)

Kayaking (K-1)

*Stationary Draw - A static stroke with the powerface deflecting oncoming water (frontal resistance) at an angle, causing the craft to move both toward the paddle and parallel to the blade. A sculling action or a dynamic draw can continue the craft's movement. Paddlers rotate their torsos to allow paddle entry into the water just aft of their bodies.

Draw - Moves the boat sideways. Reach out directly across from the hip to begin the stroke, and pull the blade toward the hip with the lower hand while the upper hand pushes. The blade slices out behind the paddler for a recovery or may be recovered under water.

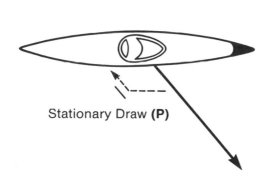

Stationary Draw (P)

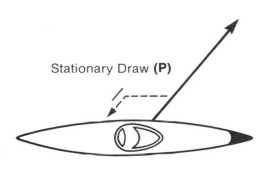

Stationary Draw (P)

Maneuvers: Turns

Tandem Canoeing (OC-2, C-2)

NOTE: The other strokes illustrated in this section are described elsewhere in this chapter.

Reverse Sweeping Low Brace (RSLB) *-* A tandem stern stroke used when the canoe is turning to the offside of the bowperson (an inside turn for the stern person). The stroke is somewhat like a modified reverse ¼ sweep where the knuckles are down (as in a low brace), but the blade is flattened against the water (45 degrees). While sweeping in a reverse arc, the paddler unweights the offside knee and leans into the turn by applying pressure to the backface of the blade. Keep the blade near the surface and extend the paddle so that both hands are over the water. When this stroke is being executed, the bowperson is usually doing either a cross Duffek or a forward ¼ sweep (the latter is more common in a decked canoe).

Reverse Sweeping Low Brace

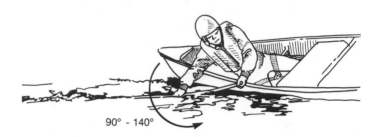

90° - 140°

Both hands remain low as the paddle sweeps from the stern, past a point directly opposite the hip. The brace is usually converted quickly to a forward stroke somewhere beyond 90° from the stern.

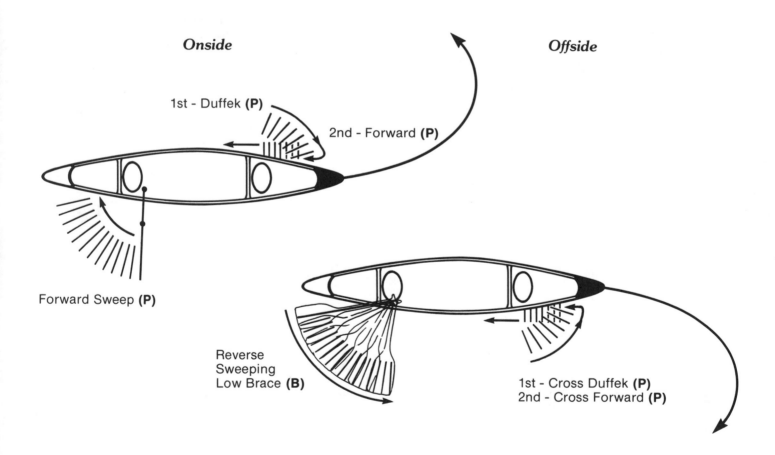

Onside

Offside

1st - Duffek **(P)**

2nd - Forward **(P)**

Forward Sweep **(P)**

Reverse Sweeping Low Brace **(B)**

1st - Cross Duffek **(P)**
2nd - Cross Forward **(P)**

Solo Canoeing (OC-1, C-1)

NOTE: The strokes illustrated in this section are described elsewhere in this chapter.

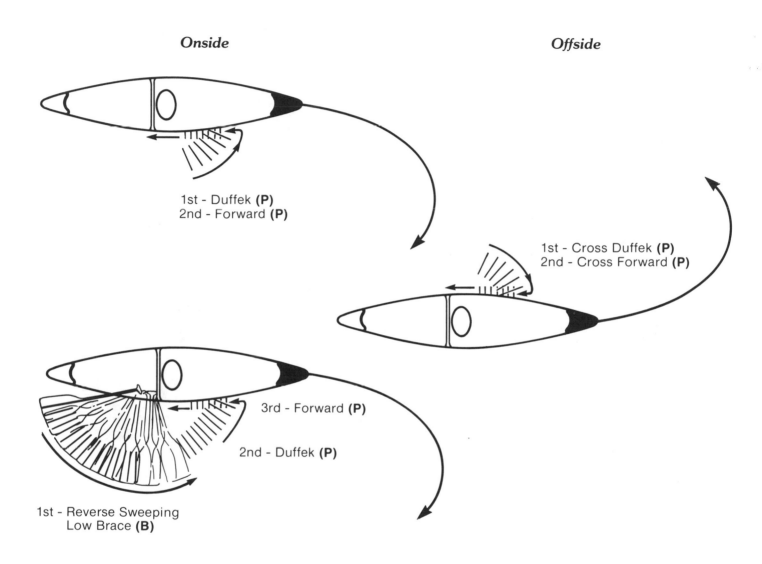

Onside

Offside

1st - Duffek **(P)**
2nd - Forward **(P)**

1st - Cross Duffek **(P)**
2nd - Cross Forward **(P)**

3rd - Forward **(P)**

2nd - Duffek **(P)**

1st - Reverse Sweeping
Low Brace **(B)**

Kayaking (K-1)

High Brace - Stabilizes and turns the boat. The paddle blade is inserted in front of or opposite the body to begin the stroke (never behind the body) with the upper hand well below the chin. A kayaker leans the boat with the knees and hips rather than leaning the body onto the paddle.

Duffek - For talented beginners, or novice and intermediate paddlers. From a forward stroke position, cock the wrists back until the paddle shaft is approximately at an 80-degree angle to the water surface. The paddle is place in the water at a 45-degree angle (sometimes larger) to the boat's centerline. The upper forearm is across the forehead with the top hand over the opposite shoulder, while the lower arm is bent. Canoeists adopted this stroke from kayakers. (See page 50 for a detailed description of the Duffek stroke)

The "low" High Brace.

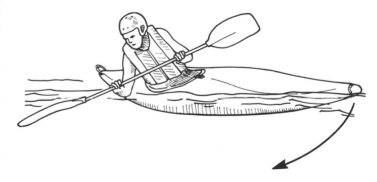

Maneuvers: Bracing

Braces are used to stablize the craft and to prevent a boat from tipping over. A bracing stroke is similar to an outrigger. Braces can be "high" or "low" depending upon the position of the shaft.

High Brace - The most common kayak and canoe brace for general stability. In a canoe the blade is inserted somewhat vertically with the knuckles of both hands up. *(See illustration)* A modified high brace position with lowered hands is a good **running position** in rapids. Stability is enhanced and other strokes can be initiated easily from this position. In a kayak the high brace is best executed in the "low" position with the elbows down and the shaft below the chin. (See the previous page for an illustration)

Low Brace - A low brace is used mostly in canoeing when the craft suddenly tips (usually from the capsizing force of a lateral opposing current) toward the paddler's side. The paddle is nearly horizontal, and the knuckles and thumbs of both hands face down; the brace or force is applied to the backface of the paddle.

In tandem paddling, one partner uses a low brace, while the other person is forced to immediately execute a dynamic high brace draw to counteract the tipping. The combination should right the boat, although it may be partially swamped. Timing is crucial.

The solo canoeist learns to favor the paddling side by creating a slight list of the craft. As in tandem paddling, the solo paddler uses a high brace for the running position. Then the paddler is prepared when a sudden list toward the paddling side demands a quick conversion to the low brace. If the boat tips excessively toward the offside, then a cross low brace can be attempted!

Turning Braces - A turning brace is executed by applying force on the powerface (turning high brace) or the backface (turning low brace) while the craft is moving forward. The angle set on the blade deflects the water and thus causes the boat to turn. See the Duffek stroke for a more detailed description of a turning high brace. See the reverse sweeping low brace for information on a turning low brace.

High Brace

The paddle remains in the water with a dynamic high brace draw which stabilizes the boat.

Low Brace

Both hands remain low and outside the boat for an effective low brace. The control hand may be lower as long as the hip snap is initiated with the blade near the water surface.

Instructor's Notebook

New Directions in U-Turns on the River

A major part of any instructional workshop is the practice of eddy turns and peelouts. These exciting maneuvers give new paddlers a sense of satisfaction and challenge. They are "playing the river" rather than allowing the river to play with them!

Eddy turns and peelouts are often called "U-turns", because the maneuvers enable a paddler to change direction in the river. The **eddy turn** allows a paddler to leave the fast current, pivot the boat and enter the relative calm of an eddy. The **peelout** allows a paddler to leave the security of that resting place in the eddy, pivot the boat and reenter the current rushing past.

U-turns can be introduced in terms of six major components:
1. Angle of boat entry or exit
2. Position of boat entry or exit
3. Forward momentum
4. Initial torque or turn
5. Boat lean
6. Strokes

1. *Angle of boat entry or exit.* For the eddy turn, the angle of entry into the eddy is 45 degrees or larger to the eddy line. The angle provides the boat with exposure to opposing currents (main current and eddy current). The currents hit the ends of the boat and turn it around. The narrower the eddy, the larger the angle of entry. A paddler can enter a small eddy almost broadside to the current. That strategy will prevent the boat from charging through the eddy (and out the other side or into a shoreline!)

For the peelout, the angle of exit from the eddy is 45 degrees or smaller to the eddy line. The angle provides the boat with exposure to the fast downstream current. This main current hits the leading end of the boat and spins it around. The faster the downstream current, the smaller the angle of exit. If a paddler enters fast current with too wide an angle, the boat spins on the eddy line (and strikes the rock or wallows on the unstable eddy line).

The angle of entry or exit is the responsibility of the paddler in the following end of a tandem canoe.

2. *Position of entry or exit.* The paddler strives to enter or exit the eddy close to the obstacle creating the eddy but with enough clearance so the pivoting boat doesn't bump the obstacle.

The eddy is strongest in the protected area behind the rock or ledge, where it holds or slows the boat. If paddlers enter lower in the eddy to turn, the hold upon the craft becomes weaker. The downriver current is pulling more of the eddy current away from the protection of the rock, and the paddler has to work harder to keep the boat in the eddy.

If leaving the eddy too low, the paddlers fail to take advantage of the strongest current differentials (between the quickest "entering" current and the "leaving" current). The peelout will be less crisp as a result.

The position of entry or exit is the responsibility of the paddler in the following end of a tandem canoe.

3. *Forward momentum.* Once the angle of entry is established for an eddy turn, the paddlers must paddle forward into the eddy. If they don't the craft will float downstream past the eddy.

On a peelout, the paddlers need forward momentum to leave the eddy and reenter the main current. Otherwise, the majority of the turn occurs in the eddy, where the paddlers do most of the work. Use enough forward momentum to get the bow into the downstream flow, and the current will perform most of the work.

The right momentum is important. Apply just enough power to partially cross the eddy line (two to three strokes). With the eddy turn, too much power will drive the boat through the eddy — out the other side or into the river bank. With the peelout, excessive power will drive both ends of the boat into the main current and does not take advantage of the opposing current differentials. (The peelout becomes a slower spin.) Guage your power to gain the advantage obtained when the boat's bow is exposed to the "entering" current, and the stern remains in the "leaving" current. The greater the current differential, the faster the boat will turn.

Momentum is the responsibility of both paddlers in a tandem canoe.

4. *Initial torque or turn.* Just before the boat slides over the eddy line, the paddler begins to spin (or "torque") the boat. Paddlers can execute the proper stroke with a downstream lean, but they must shift the boat lean immediately after the torque stroke and just prior to the craft crossing the eddy line. This torque is not necessary if the boat is already turning properly. It reduces the force or pressure on the shoulders of the paddler when the Duffek stroke is executed.

The initial torque is the responsibility of the paddler in the following end of a tandem canoe.

5. *Boat lean.* As soon as the bow of the boat slides over the eddy line, the paddlers must lean into the u-turn like they are riding a bicycle. The greater the difference between the speed of the "leaving" current and the speed of the "entering" current, the greater the lean.

By leaning the boat, the paddlers present the bottom of the boat to the onrushing "entering" current. The lean reduces the water's tug or "catch" on the edge of the boat. The action fights the tendency of the boat to be tipped to the outside of the turn.

The greatest cause of tipping during a peelout is paddlers who fail to provide adequate lean.

By leaning the boat on its bilge, the paddler increases the rocker of the boat. The ends of the craft are lifted higher from the water and water resistance against the boat is minimized. As a result, the boat will turn more easily.

Boat lean in canoes and kayaks is created with pressure from their lower bodies. Paddlers lean their bodies only slightly. To avoid an exaggerated body lean, the weight is shifted smoothly onto one knee or one hip, and the pressure rolls the boat onto its side or edge under the paddler.

Both paddlers in a tandem canoe must provide boat lean.

6. *Strokes.* The turning strokes are the last and least important step to execute. If every preceding step is executed properly, turning strokes are often unnecessary.

An Eddy

CURRENT DIRECTION

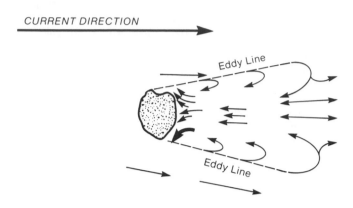

U-Turns

CURRENT DIRECTION

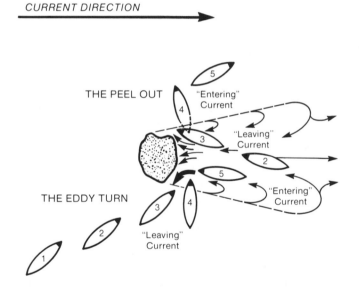

THE PEEL OUT

"Entering" Current

"Leaving" Current

THE EDDY TURN

"Entering" Current

"Leaving" Current

- *Develop entering momentum at position 2.*
- *Begin the initial torque at position number 3.*
- *Must lean downstream to the entering current as soon as the "entering end" of the boat crosses the eddy line.*
- *A turning brace (i.e. duffek) is placed in the entering current. This brace should initially broach the entering current. If entering the eddy high, this means the powerface is almost at a right angle to the boat since the entering current is flowing out (see dark arrow above).*

Use of turning strokes occurs after the bow of the boat crashes the eddy line. For an eddy turn, the paddler places the blade in the calm water just behind the obstacle. The blade becomes the point around which the boat pivots. By placing the blade perpendicular to the "entering" current, it acts as a stopper against the water (see diagram of eddy currents).

For the peelout, the paddle functions as a pivot point also. As the bow slides out into the downstream current, the paddler places the blade perpendicular to the "entering" current for maximum support.

Because Duffek strokes provide stability and turning action, they are the preferred strokes for tandem bow paddlers, solo canoeists and kayakers. However, beginners can feel uncomfortable with the Duffek initially and may need to experiment with "low" high braces.

Duffek strokes are usually converted into a forward stroke when the bow moves to the paddle. With the eddy turn, these combination strokes keep the boat from drifting out of the eddy. With the peelout, the forward stroke helps to propel the boat downriver after the craft has turned.

The key is to execute the strokes in a smooth, continuous manner. One continuous sequence of strokes is more efficient than the more jerky repetition of one stroke.

In canoeing, U-turns are described as "on-side" or "off-side" manuevers. The point of reference is the bow or solo paddler and the designated paddling side of those paddlers (the side of the boat where they execute forward strokes). An "on-side" turn or peelout refers to a U-turn where the boat is turning in the direction of the canoeist's paddling side. An "offside" eddy turn or peelout refers to a U-turn where the canoe turns away from the paddler's designated side.

Tandem canoeists (OC-2) paddle most effectively when executing turning and power strokes in unison. Because of the responsiveness of their craft, C-2 paddlers can use differing types of strokes for different effects. For instance, one partner can plant the paddle as an "anchor," holding it stationary, while the other paddler executes turning strokes. A quick, crisp turn results.

Solo canoeists (OC-1, C-1) and kayakers paddle most efficiently through U-turns when they act as "bow" paddlers. Good power and turning action occurs. But some situations may call for stern strokes. For instance, a paddler who enters an eddy with excessive speed may need a reverse sweeping low brace to slow the boat as it turns. Otherwise, the boat may slide through the eddy and out again.

This special "Instructor's Notebook" was originally published in *The American Canoeist* newsletter as part of a series of informational updates. Look for additional articles on special topics of interest to instructors.

Offside Eddy Turn

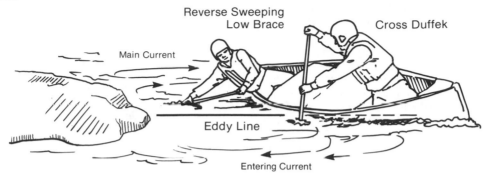

Reverse Sweeping Low Brace

Cross Duffek

Main Current

Eddy Line

Entering Current

Offside Peelout

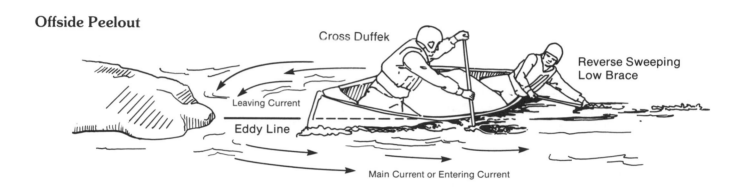

Cross Duffek

Reverse Sweeping Low Brace

Leaving Current

Eddy Line

Main Current or Entering Current

On Side Eddy Turn

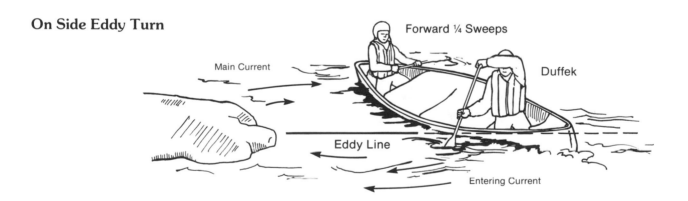

Forward ¼ Sweeps

Duffek

Main Current

Eddy Line

Entering Current

Onside Peelout

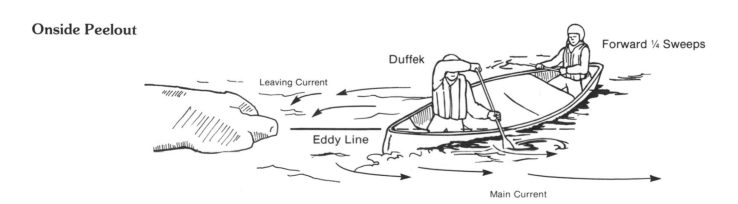

Forward ¼ Sweeps

Duffek

Leaving Current

Eddy Line

Main Current

Maneuvers: Ferries

Ferries are one of the most frequently used paddling maneuvers. They move the boat from one side of the river to another, from one channel to a new one and from one eddy to another. They are effective in enabling paddlers to scout rapids from different vantages.

Ferries require that beginners understand two principles: the boat must be moving slower than the current and at an angle to it for a ferry to work. When a boat is angled against the current (rather than parallel to and aligned with the current), the rushing water strikes the boat's upstream side or edge and pushes it. The stronger the current and the more angled the boat, the quicker the boat will move. The boat must be moving slower than the downstream current to move to the side. Otherwise, its forward momentum would continue to push it downriver.

The principles of ferries are essentially the same for canoes and kayaks. However, the maneuverability of various boats will affect how quickly or strongly paddlers must act in order to execute the ferries.

The two basic types are:

1. **a back (downstream) ferry** — paddler(s) are facing downstream and back paddling to slow the boat's descent.

2. **a forward (upstream) ferry** — paddler(s) are facing upstream and paddling forward to slow the boat's descent.

The steps to perform a ferry are similar for both types.

1. Choose a destination across the river.

2. Change the boat's alignment *with* the current to an angle *against* it. The angle will vary with current speed, the distance between the boat, the destination, and the speed with which paddlers want to reach the destination.

When the boat has a narrow angle against the current (5 to 20 degrees), less of the craft is exposed to the current. The boat points more upstream, and lateral movement will be slower.

When the boat has a wider angle against the current (20 to almost 80 degrees), more of the craft is exposed to the current. The boat points more toward the destination, and lateral movement will be quicker.

3. Slow the craft's descent by paddling forward or backward. Hold or modify the boat's position depending upon its closeness to the destination. The intensity of the paddling may change, if the boat begins to climb upriver (in mild current) or to float downriver (in strong current).

4. The upstream end of the boat enters the "destination" eddy or channel first.

Maintaining the boat's angle against the current is helped with an awareness of physical resistances (see *Chapter 7: Strokes*). The boat is traveling slower than the current, and the current's greatest force is against the upstream end. The eddy-resistance end (or end with the least lateral resistance) is the downstream end. As a result, changing the boat's angle is most *effective* near the downstream end where **turning** strokes can be executed. Maintaining position in the river (to prevent sliding downstream) is most *effective* in the upstream end, where **power** strokes can be executed.

The implications for tandem paddlers are important. Generally, the paddler in the upstream end provides power, and the partner in the downstream end turns the boat if needed *and* provides power.

Leaving an eddy to perform a ferry can be tricky. Beginners often leave the eddy with too wide an angle (and little downstream lean). Tips often occur at the start of the maneuver, after the current strikes the boat and spins it abruptly.

With practice, new paddlers will develop a sensitivity for entering a "destination" eddy. A subtle shift in boat lean is required from the downstream (or "leaving") current to the eddy ("entering" or upstream) current. With extreme current differentials, paddlers who fail to change their boat lean as they enter the eddy will often tip in the eddy.

The greater the maneuverability of a boat, the easier it spins out of a ferry position. Paddlers need to practice ferries to become familiar with the timing required in setting and maintaining ferry positions.

Many beginners find that upstream ferries are easier to practice because forward strokes provide good power for maintaining position in the river. Back ferries are often more frustrating for tandem paddlers because the "downstream" paddler can be unaware of the boat's angle in relation to the current. Maintaining the angle can be difficult and requires repeated practice.

Forward Ferry

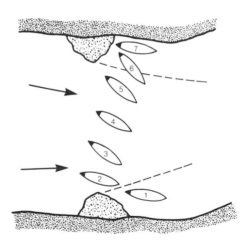

Back Ferry

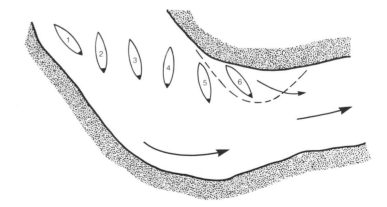

Maneuvers: Kayak Rolling

A modified "screw" roll or a modified "C-to-C" roll is a two-part process using a sweep stroke combined with a hip snap. The sweep brings the paddler's body from under the boat and up to the water's surface in a "C" position. Then the lower body can snap the boat upright with a hip snap to the second "C" position. The roll is effortless when done properly.

While a roll has many variations, this roll is an effective one for students because:

1. the set-up is quick
2. it is effective in flatwater and aerated water
3. stress upon the body is reduced (when performed efficiently)
4. the execution is quick (2 to 3 seconds)

The Hip Snap is composed of a flip of the hip and an upward thrust of the leg on the side where one is rolling up. An essential element of the hip snap is keeping the head from breaking the water's surface first. The parts of the body that break the surface (in order) are the waist, torso, shoulders and head. A good hip snap is critical to a good roll.

Exercise: The paddlers place their hands on top of a friend's hands or the bow of a boat. Rock the boat slightly toward the friend and hip snap it back to a level position. Paddlers should rock farther and farther over, until they are upside down. They should strive for minimal downward pressure against the friend's hands to make the hip snap do the work.

The Sweep is executed from a set-up position, where the paddler moves the paddle in an arch from the bow to opposite one's torso.

The set-up position is determined by the side upon which the paddler plans to roll up. (It will be the side where the hip snap feels best.) For descriptive purposes in this article, the paddler is learning to roll up on the right side.

First, the paddler grips the shaft as he or she is taking a forward stroke on the right side. Without shifting the grip on the paddle, the paddler swings the right blade over to the opposite side of the boat. The right paddle blade rests on the deck at the same sloping angle as the front left deck. The powerface of the paddler's blade faces up.

Exercise: Practice setting up several times, until the paddler is comfortable with settling quickly into the right set-up position.

The difficult stage is the underwater path of the paddle, as it moves toward the water surface. Paddlers often experience an initial disorientation when overturned.

Exercise: The paddler needs the help of a friend (wearing a helmet) who will wade into the water and support the paddler. The friend braces himself well on the same side of the anticipated roll (i.e. friend on right side if rolling up on right). He supports the paddler with a loose hug around the chest (under the armpits) and lowers the paddler (right shoulder down) to the water.

The relaxed paddler (with eyes above the water) moves the paddle from the set-up position and sweeps it across the surface of the water. When the paddle reaches a point that is almost perpendicular to the boat (75 to 90 degrees to the centerline), the paddler executes the hip snap. Be sure the paddle does not sweep behind the body.

The Set-Up

Wrist cocking of hand nearest the bow at the set up.

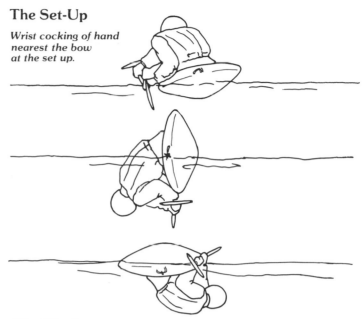

The Hip Snap

Begin the hip snap as the paddle blade sweeps out to 90°. Boat should be upright when paddle reaches 90°. Hands do not move behind the upper body plane.

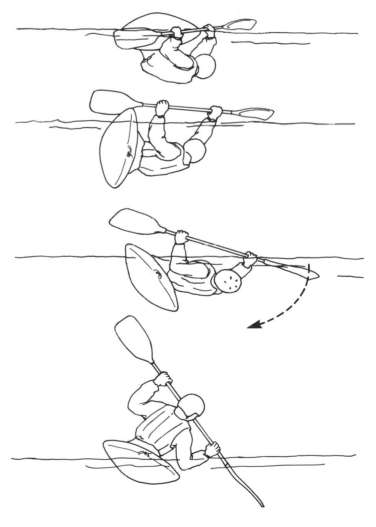

A common inefficiency may be inadequate cocking of the wrists, when setting up the paddle blade (or the paddle dives to the river bottom); the paddle blade angle should be just slightly off a parallel position to the water surface (so it climbs and stays on top of the water). Over-cocking of the wrists will make the paddle plow and slowly dive.

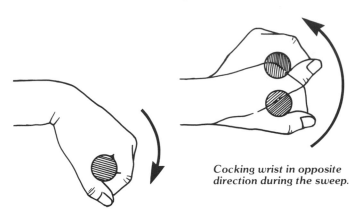

Cocking wrist in opposite direction during the sweep.

Wrist cocking at setting up.

As the paddler sweeps the paddle in the arc, he must increase smoothly the cocking of the wrist. The change in the wrists changes the blade angle and maintains its climbing ability to the water's surface.

For the initial rolling attempts, the friend can continue to assist the paddler until he develops a feel for the sweep of the paddle. After tipping over to the right, the friend can sweep the paddle around while the paddler sets up and hip snaps at the beginning and end of the roll. With each tip, the paddler will take over more control of the sweep until he is rolling with no help.

Another common inefficiency can be failure to take the time to set up properly by positioning the paddle on the water surface next to the boat before starting to sweep out.

A paddler who is failing to roll effortlessly must analyze his actions early and correct the problem before bad habits develop. By taping a large two-inch-thick piece of ethafoam to the paddle blade, a paddler is nearly guaranteed that he will roll up. Then he can work on the problem area of the roll without worrying about rolling up.

Common Problems

Problem: Blade starts to dive about one-third of the way through the sweep.
Cause: Failure to cock wrists during sweep.
Solution: Cock wrists gradually throughout the sweep.

Problem: Blade diving straight to bottom.
Cause: Poor paddle angle (wrists are too cocked) or pulling the paddle.
Solution: Cock wrists downward at the start of the sweep. Reach and extend the paddle so that both hands break the water surface during the sweep. Make sure the blade starts the sweep when it is on top of the water surface.

Problem: Non-sweeping blade is hitting the boat.
Cause: Blade not being brought over the hull of the boat.
Solution: Stick the non-sweeping hand up out of the water at the start of the sweep.

Problem: Poor hip snap
Cause: Concentration on the sweep and forgetting to hip snap. Timing of the hip snap is too early or too late. Bringing the head and/or shoulder out of the water first.
Solution: Hip snap when the paddle is between 75 and 90 degrees to the boat. The slower the hip snap, the sooner the paddler should start it. The paddler should put her chin on her shoulder or bite the lifejacket to keep the head coming up last. In a sequence, bring up the torso, shoulders and then the head.

Problem: Paddle dives when the hip snap occurs
Cause: 1. Pulling down on the blade rather than emphasizing the hip snap. 2. Pushing up toward the sky with the non-sweeping arm. 3. Pulling the arms into the side when rushing the sweep.
Solution: 1. Practice hip snaps without the paddle and emphasize reaching out and up during the sweep. 2. Keep the elbow below shoulder level and bring the arm across the chest. 3. Reach out and up with the sweeping arm.

Problem: Falling out of the boat
Cause: 1. Failure to brace legs against the boat. 2. Lack of tight outfitting in the boat.
Solution: 1. Stiffen legs when tipping to counter the pull of gravity. 2. Check the footbrace length and seat padding at the hips.

Dangerous Problems

Problem: Shoulder dislocation or stressed muscles and ligaments.
Cause: 1. Letting the paddle sweep beyond the body. 2. Using the paddle to right the boat instead of the hip snap. 3. Using a hip snap too late.

Problem: Hip snapping off the back deck which puts a paddler's head and face in a vulnerable position if the roll fails.
Cause: A backward body lean or swing to the stern
Solution: Tuck upper body to deck when tipping over to protect the head and face from the rocks.

Decked Canoe Rolling

Two common styles are used in C-1 and C-2 rolling: an onside roll (also known as a low-brace roll) and an offside roll.

C-1 and C-2 rolls can be similar if both paddlers set up on the same side and develop a system of coordinating with each other. This style is powerful, but it requires that one paddler switch sides quickly upon completion of the roll to counter balance the move. Otherwise, C-2 paddlers use differing rolls; one executes an offside roll while the other uses an onside roll. The latter technique is less common because the offside roll is more difficult. (It will not be described in this manual).

The Onside Roll

This roll is similar to a "C to C" kayaking roll in the set-up and hip snap, but the bracing changes from a high brace to low brace position during the execution.

If paddlers fall over on a brace, they can keep the blade of the paddle near the surface. As the boat tips upside down, the torso sinks only slightly and the torso is curled upwards into a "C" position. The blade of the paddle is near the surface and is swept upwards in a high brace position to clear the surface.

The roll is executed by hip snapping (flipping the hip) and pulling the knee nearest the paddle when upright toward the chest. As the boat flips from upside down to right side up, the paddler executes a sweeping movement of the blade (low brace position) toward the front of the boat. As the blade sweeps, the head and torso move from the side of the boat and in the water to the front of the boat and above the water.

Exercise: Put the paddle in the start position along the front edge of the boat. The blade is flat against the deck (parallel to the surface of the deck) with the blade toward the bow and the control hand near the cowling of the cockpit. The shaft should be parallel to the keel of the boat. The backface of the blade is against the deck.

Practice the set-up several times while upright. Then tip over with the blade out of the position and practice moving the paddle through the water to the right position.

Exercise: Rotate the torso and paddle from the deck to an outstretched position with the blade near or at the water surface (a 90-degree position from the centerline). The sweeping rotation occurs in a high brace position (the powerface down and the thumb of the grip hand pointed toward the body). The torso is curled in a "C" so the head is in the water but near the surface while the cockpit is down.

Paddlers may need a friend to help sweep the blade toward the surface. (Note use of friend in kayak roll description.)

Exercise: Convert from the high brace to a low brace by rotating the control thumb up and away from body. The control hand is moving from the surface to a deeper position under the floating torso. The blade remains at or near the surface

Exercise: The hip snap moves the boat from the cockpit-down position to an upright position. While upside down, push on the knee nearest the torso and pull the knee farthest away. At the same time, contract the muscles on the side nearest the river bottom.

A partner can help snap the boat (see description for kayak rolling) to improve the crispness of the hip snap.

Exercise: Complete the roll with a low brace to bring the body and head into a balanced position over the boat. Keep the center of gravity low by bending forward at the waist and maintaining a "climbing" angle (backface down) on the paddle so that it supports the body weight. Straighten the torso when the boat is balanced. As in kayaking, bring up the torso, shoulders and then the head.

Common Problems

Generally, paddlers encounter the same problems as kayakers during the high brace phase (see previous section). But additional problems may occur.

A special problem stems from the kneeling position (and the paddler's greater distance from the boat). C-1 and C-2 paddlers sustain greater pressure on the arms and shoulders during the roll. They must convert quickly to a low brace to complete the roll.

If paddlers fail to continue the forward sweeping low brace, they will stall and fall back into the water.

C-2 Rolls

Coordination is the key to successful C-2 rolling. Teams develop a sensitivity to each other and can match their rolling actions through subtle signals.

One partner can wait in the first "C" position until he feels the other paddler initiate the hip snap and then join in quickly. It involves little wasted time and is the preferred technique.

A less subtle approach involves one person tapping the boat while upside down to begin the sequence. Both paddlers may also begin the paddle sweep on pre-arranged count system. These processes involves more time upside down and partners can fail to hear the signal.

RIVER READING

Chapter IX

River Reading is a Skill

Knowing how water flows downhill is the key to river reading. Studying currents is a necessary exercise, and the application of that knowledge to the river environment is often difficult. Water in a river can look chaotic, especially to a beginner, and it's only through experience that a paddler develops river reading skills.

Inexperienced paddlers should begin to develop river reading skills in mild current before they attempt more difficult rapids. Scouting from shore is helpful to allow more time to study the currents, but a paddler must learn to recognize its characteristics from both high and low vantage points. The lower level is more akin to the perspective a paddler encounters when looking from a boat.

An instructor should acquaint students with the fundamentals of river currents as a means of developing river-reading skills. Once a paddler learns to recognize downstream V's, rolling waves, rooster tails and eddy lines, the river world becomes a more familiar place. With this understanding, a paddler develops an increased sense of comfort and an ability to take greater advantage of the opportunities that a river offers.

Teaching Methods: Exercises vary from "classroom style" introductions to at-the-river presentations: blackboard diagrams, an "indoor" river (with rocks, strainers and other hazards) upon which students can move small boats and discuss river reading, a small stream that has "miniature" river hydraulics or a river site with a variety of currents and obstacles.

Fundamentals of River Currents

Water is "lazy" in that it flows downhill continuously until an obstacle forces it in a different direction. Water generally seeks the easiest descent — the steepest, clearest route within the riverbed.

Current speed or **velocity** is affected by the volume of water, river width, and gradient.

Volume is the amount of flowing water, often expressed in cubic feet per second (cfs). The greater the volume of water, the faster it flows.

Gradient is the steepness of the riverbed, often expressed in feet per mile. The steepness is characterized by two conditions — rapids and pools. A **rapid** is a steeper incline with faster current that is generally shallower in depth. A **pool** is a lesser-inclined section of the river with slower current and deeper water.

The steeper the terrain, the faster the river flows. The head of a rapid is often slower than the middle or lower section. As fast current meets slower current (ie. at a pool), it is slowed abruptly and often forms waves.

A Pool

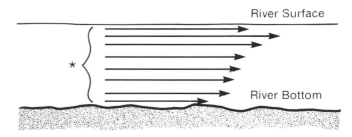

Obstacles can be hidden just beneath the surface.

Width. A decrease in river width funnels the river into a constriction. Converging currents slam together and often create turbulence.

Current can also be affected by other variables. Water moves slower near the river bottom because of friction with the riverbed. The faster water is nearer the surface, where friction is less. The edge of a river will sometimes show boils of water from friction against the banks.

Side View of a River

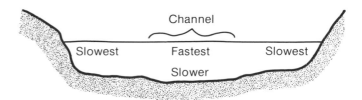

Arrow length indicates relative current speed.

The fastest water is just beneath the surface. Friction with air and the river bottom creates slower water.

As a river bends, the water tends to be faster and deeper near the outside of the bend. Water hitting the outside bend creates a deep channel and a river bank that is often eroding and undercut. It can be jammed with trees called **strainers** that have toppled into the river; the tree branches allow the passage of water but they often trap boats or people.

The inside of the bend has the slowest, shallowest water. It may be so shallow that rocks or **shoals,** rocky banks or bars, are exposed just off the shore.

Straight River

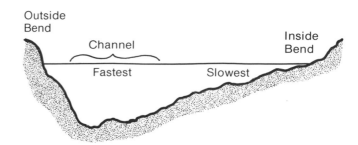

River Bend

The Effects of Obstacles

Current within the river is a function of the geology around and in the river. The contours of the riverbed and obstacles within it force current to move in various directions. If the geology of an area is primarily jagged ledges with steep contours, then the character of that river will be very different from a river that meanders through farmland in a wide valley.

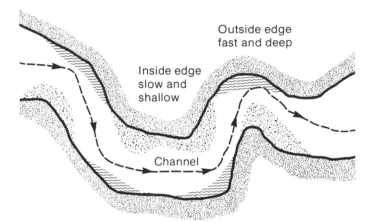

The channel flows to the outside of the riverbends and often bounces away from the bank in irregular patterns.

Deeper channels are created between obstacles as the water bounces off the rocks and flows around them. The lines of current meet in the channel as a **downstream V.**

Deeper, slow-moving water will move easily over and around obstacles with little disturbance on the surface, and the V's will appear smooth. But quicker water and larger obstacles can disturb that smooth surface and create chaotic whitewater conditions. The V's will be more turbulent and look like peaking waves. Paddlers need to examine the V's carefully, because even the best route can be choked by a rock that forces them to alter their course within the V.

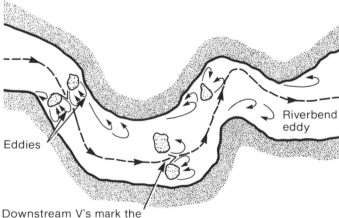

Downstream V's mark the channel between obstacles.

In slower current, a rock just under the surface will create a disturbance just downstream of it, often in the form of a tightly curling wave. The rock becomes an obstacle called a **pillow,** because of the smooth sheen of water covering the rock.

In slower current, a rock just above the surface will force the water to flow around it. The smoother area of water behind the obstacle is an **eddy.** If the eddy water is dark and stable, it is a **black eddy.** If the eddy water is aerated, lighter in color and less stable, it is a **white eddy.** An eddy that is bubbling up from beneath the obstacle is a **boiling eddy** and often is caused by an undercut rock. The rock is usually narrower at its base, and current flows beneath a portion of it to disturb the eddy.

Any of these eddies are a haven of more protected water in the midst of the river. They provide a stopping spot where paddlers can scout their next route.

In faster and deeper current, a rock will create a bigger, more peaked wave a little farther downstream called a **standing wave.** Very well-formed peaks that are breaking slightly are know as **haystacks.**

In very fast and very deep current, a larger rock will create a more rolling wave like surf preparing to break at the ocean. These **breaking waves** can swamp an open boat or change drastically the course of any boat.

Current at Lower Water

Small reversals are created downstream of obstacles.

Current at Higher Water

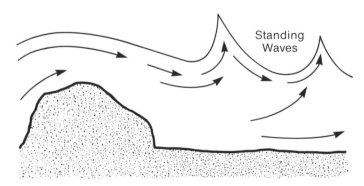

Pillows are covered by deeper water and waves are formed farther downstream.

Fast, deep water can drop sharply over an extremely large obstacle into a depression known as a **hole, hydraulic** or **reversal**. The volume isn't great enough to flow over the ledge or rock and continue downriver in the form of waves. The water gets trapped in the depression below the large rock, recirculates upstream and continues to roll around within the deep hole.

The more foaming and aerated the water in a hole, the less buoyancy the water will give. A boat will sink down into the hole and have difficulty leaving it. The stronger the flow of recirculating water, the more difficult it will be to paddle through and out of the hole. A large hole with very strong upstream current is called a **keeper**, because it will hold boats in it.

A Hole

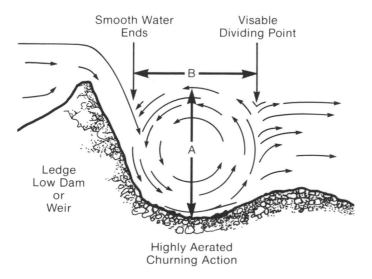

The depth of a hole (A) is often equal to the width of the boiling water (B), the latter of which can usually be determined visually.

Open boat paddlers run the risk of swamping in holes, while decked boaters may capsize. Paddlers caught in a hole should swim to either end, where downstream current will help pull them from the hole. An alternative is to catch the current leaving the hole and flowing downstream. Holes deserve the respect of boaters, for a trapped paddler can become disoriented when caught in the recirculating current.

A Good Rule: *The length of a hole can be equal to its depth.* Holes longer than four feet are considered very strong, often dangerous holes.

Man-made obstacles like dams and weirs often have a uniform hole at their base that extends across the entire river width. These extremely regular holes are large and life-threatening, because escape from them is limited and often impossible.

The appearance of a **horizon line**, where only the top of the scenery downstream is evident, is clear evidence of a dam or natural ledge. Other signs are increased noise from falling water and spray or mist from the impact of the drop. Proceed with caution and be prepared to stop to scout the drop.

International Scale of River Difficulty

The American Whitewater Affiliation's *International Scale of River Difficulty* is a useful tool to determine the severity of sections in a river. These guidelines offer a general classification for rivers, but be aware that the system is not exact. Rivers do not always fit neatly into the various classifications, and regional interpretations of the classification system may create misunderstandings.

There is no substitute for a cautious approach to rivers with which a paddler is unfamiliar.

Moving water has three classifications:
1. Class A   Flowing under 2 m.p.h.
2. Class B   2 to 4 m.p.h.
3. Class C   Greater than 4 m.p.h.

Whitewater has six classifications:

Class I: Easy
- Few or no obstructions — all obvious and easily missed
- Fast-moving water with riffles and small waves
- Risk to swimmers is slight
- Self-rescue is easy

Class II: Novice
- Straightforward rapids with wide, clear channels that are obvious without scouting
- Occasional maneuvering may be required but rocks and medium-sized waves are missed easily by trained paddlers
- Swimmers are seldom injured and group assistance, while helpful, is seldom needed

Class III: Intermediate
- Rapids with moderate, irregular waves which may be difficult to avoid and capable of swamping an open canoe
- Complex maneuvers in fast current and narrow passages requiring good boat control frequently exist
- Large waves, holes and strainers may be present but are easily avoided
- Strong eddies and powerful current effects can be found, particularly on large-volume rivers
- Scouting is advisable for inexperienced parties
- Chances of injury while swimming is low, but group assistance may be required to avoid long swims.

Class IV: Advanced
- Intense, powerful rapids requiring precise boat handling in turbulent water
- Depending upon the character of the river, there may be long unavoidable waves and holes or constricted passages demanding fast maneuvers under pressure
- A fast, reliable eddy turn may be needed to negotiate the drop, scout rapids or rest
- Rapids may require "must" moves above dangerous hazards
- Scouting is necessary the first time
- Risk of injury to swimmers is moderate to high, and water conditions may make rescue difficult
- Group assistance is often essential but requires practiced skills
- A strong Eskimo roll is highly recommended

Class V: Expert

- Extremely long, obstructed or violent rapids which expose the paddler to above average risk of injury
- Drops may contain very large, unavoidable waves and holes or steep, congested chutes with complex, demanding routes
- Rapids often continue for long distances between pools or eddies, demanding a high level of fitness
- What eddies exist may be small, turbulent or difficult to reach
- Several of these factors may be combined at the high end of this class
- Scouting is mandatory
- Rescue is extremely difficult even for experts
- A very reliable Eskimo roll and above-average rescue skills are essential

Class VI: Almost Impossible

- Difficulties of Class V are carried to the limits of navigability
- Nearly impossible and very dangerous
- Risks are high and rescue may be impossible
- For teams of experts only at favorable water levels, after close study and with all precautions
- The frequency with which a rapid is run should have no effect on this rating as there are a number of Class VI rapids which are regularly attempted

Factors that Affect River Classification

The international scale is a general guideline that can be affected by more specific qualifications. For instance, guidebooks will list a particular river as a "Class II" river or perhaps a "Class II-III." Within the general classification, the river may contain easier or more difficult rapids. Paddlers will often refer to a specific section as a "Class IV" drop.

Paddlers attempting difficult rapids in an unfamiliar area should exercise caution until they understand how a rating scale is interpreted locally. Because rivers may change from year to year (or between trips), paddlers must also exercise caution on familiar rivers.

Rivers can be affected by geologic disturbances, downed trees, weather and changing water conditions. Flooding or dam releases can change water levels abruptly, and paddlers must be aware of the effect of those fluctuations upon the river they are paddling. Some medium-difficulty rapids can become life-threatening situations under high water conditions, while a difficult rocky rapid can be washed out by high water and contain only large waves.

Other environmental factors can affect a river classification:

- the presence or absence of a nearby road to effect evacuation in the event of an accident
- cold weather or cold water (extra care is indicated when the water temperature drops below 50 degrees F)

River Reading Responsibilities

Reading a river is a two-part process. First, paddlers must select a safe general course within the entire river (river left, center or river right as one looks downstream). Secondly, they must avoid specific obstacles within the general course.

In a tandem canoe, the general route choice is the responsibility of both paddlers. Often, the canoeist who is farther upstream in the craft can see the entire scene more clearly. The paddler in the downstream end of the boat is closest to the obstacles and selects the immediate route.

In reading the river, paddlers will vary in their overall route choices, depending upon their paddling abilities and their style of paddling. The most important consideration in river reading is choosing a route that matches a paddler's skills.

Paddlers are advised to choose routes that allow them to paddle in control and to rescue themselves. Their skills should be sufficient to stop or reach shore before reaching danger. Paddlers are also advised to enter a rapid only if they judge that they can run it safely and swim it without injury. The ultimate responsibility for paddling a particular river stretch rests with the individuals, regardless of advice they may receive from other paddlers.

According to the American Whitewater Affiliation *Safety Code,* individuals must assume sole responsibility for the following decisions:

- evaluation of personal ability and expected difficulty of the rapids
- selection of appropriate equipment, including a boat design suited to personal skills and appropriate rescue and survival gear
- scouting any rapid (other members may offer advice, but paddlers must resist pressure from anyone to paddle beyond their skills)
- running or portaging a scouted river section (it is a personal responsibility to decide whether to pass up a walk-out or take-out opportunity)
- constant evaluation of their own and the group's situation, voicing concerns and ideas whenever appropriate and following what they believe to be the safest course of action

Paddlers must have a frank knowledge of their boating ability and the strength of their team in tandem paddling. Lesser-skilled paddlers should be paired with more talented people. Paddlers must:

- determine whether a rapid or river is beyond their abilities
- develop paddling skills and teamwork that match the rapids to be paddled
- develop skills gradually and understand that attempts to advance too quickly will compromise safety and enjoyment
- be in good physical and mental condition consistent with difficulties which may be expected
- make adjustments for loss of skills due to age, health and fitness
- explain health problems to paddlers in their group prior to beginning the program or trip

Paddlers often have different priorities in selecting routes through rapids. Enthusiastic recreational paddlers often "play the river" by executing numerous maneuvers as they move downriver. These paddlers often deliberately broach their boats to the current (turn it sideways across the river) as they paddle between obstacles. They will be searching for the more exciting current in the river.

Wilderness trippers, however, choose more cautious routes that keep them away from obstacles and in alignment with the current. A danger exists in broaching a loaded boat to the current, since the boat could become pinned against obstacles and the weight of gear would inhibit rescue efforts.

Inexperienced paddlers often fail to read the river downstream far enough to choose the best route and to avoid obstacles. Reading the river is helped by:

- looking downriver to the farthest visible point, before the river flows out of sight. Find the best channel and follow it back upriver to the boat
- repeating the first step constantly
- taking action immediately to move the boat into the proper channel
- communicating a plan of action if paddling a tandem craft
- being prepared to stop to scout a section, if the river disappears from sight, a horizon line appears or the water is too chaotic to read
- making a personal decision about running a rapid after analyzing route choices
- being aware of the entire river environment in the event that a rescue must be executed. Know the safe shore for a possible self-rescue

If paddlers fail to keep their boats in alignment with the current in the face of oncoming obstacles, the boats run the risk of broaching against the obstacle. Beginning paddlers often broach their boats by failing to see obstacles, selecting a route around an obstacle too late or failing to communicate a plan of action clearly with a partner.

When paddlers broach their boats, they should:

- lean downstream into the obstacle to avoid pinning
- elevate the upstream gunwale in an open boat to prevent the current from pulling the side down and under the water
- present the bottom of a closed craft to the current for the same reason
- pivot the craft off the obstacle by turning with the current
- prepare to leave the craft, if the boat begins to pin against the obstacle
- exit the craft to a safe position: on top of the obstacle, in the eddy behind it, to another boat. Avoid stepping upstream in strong current, because a paddler can be knocked off balance, swept under the boat and possibly pinned underwater

Two difficult broaches are the:

Amidship Broach. The boat pins at its pivot point which makes pivoting off the obstacle very difficult. Assistance is often required to keep a decked boat paddler's head above water or to remove a pinned boat.

Double End Broach. Both ends of the craft are stuck against rocks that prevent a pivoting off them. If a paddler fails to lean downstream, the boat swamps and paddlers can get caught beneath the craft and the river bottom. Quick-acting paddlers can leave the craft, and from the safety of the obstacle, they can lift one end over it. The current will then help the paddlers to pull the other end off the second rock.

Running the River

River running is a skill that takes many miles of practice to perfect. The art of reading the river is the first step, and the next step is gaining experience in executing maneuvers in the river. A paddler must develop good strategies for negotiating

rapids and then run the river using good technical skills and knowledge.

Paddlers need to observe basic river running responsibilities:

1. *Do not boat out of control.* Paddling skills must be sufficient to allow paddlers to reach shore before reaching danger.

2. *Do not attempt rapids beyond your abilities.* Paddlers should be reasonably sure that they can run a rapid safely and swim it without injury if they capsize.

3. *Evaluate your physical and mental condition constantly and match your performance to the difficulty of the rapids.* Paddlers should decide the best course of action for themselves at the moment.

Broaches

Amidship Broach

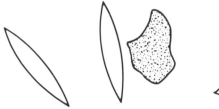

Double End Broach

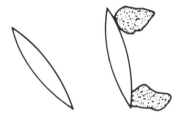

Broach in a Strainer

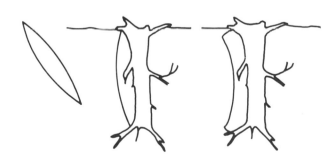

CURRENT DIRECTION →

Two basic strategies exist for river running: *a conservative approach* and *aggressive play*.

Running rapids in a conservative manner generally means traveling slower than the current or at the same speed. The approach is often used by wilderness trippers with loaded boats. Recreational boaters will also use conservative strategies to scout unfamiliar or highly technical drops.

These paddlers will often choose a less risky, slower path by using maneuvers that require back paddling. Back paddling gives paddlers more time to scout rapids, to make decisions about routes or to make corrections to their course.

Conservative Approach

Backferrying is a conservative way for paddlers to negotiate a rapid. Paddlers hug the safest shore and avoid deep, fast channels.

Common conservative strategies include:
- back ferrying around the inside of river bends
- sideslipping around rocks
- setting (back ferrying) into eddies
- backpaddling through standing waves to let the boat ride up over waves instead of diving through them

Running rapids in a more aggressive manner generally means traveling as fast and faster than the current. River runs are more thrilling, because the action is happening quickly and paddlers need to make quick decisions. These paddlers are "playing the river" by taking advantage of current to execute a variety of maneuvers. They can play hard in short sections of the river and often paddle upriver by hopping eddies to repeat a run. While they often don't paddle many miles downriver, they have actually paddled many miles within the short stretch of river.

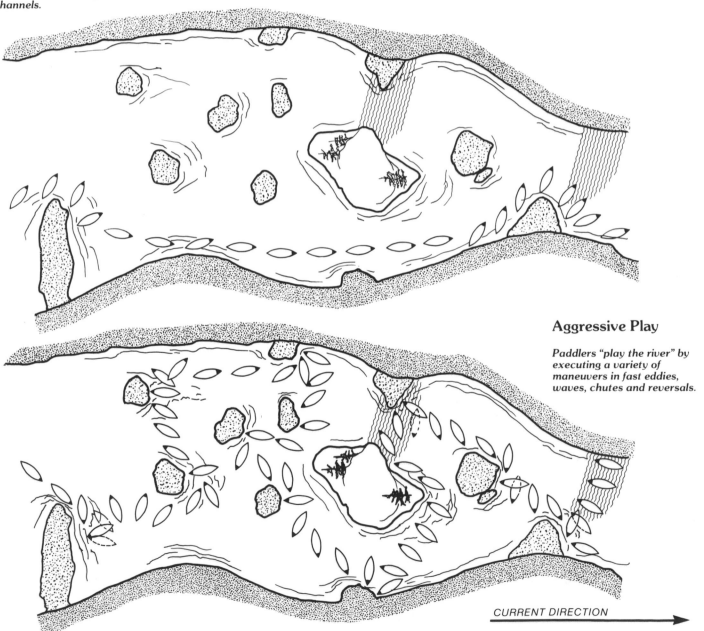

Aggressive Play

Paddlers "play the river" by executing a variety of maneuvers in fast eddies, waves, chutes and reversals.

CURRENT DIRECTION

This aggressive approach frequently requires that paddlers use forward power to execute their maneuvers. They often deliberately choose the fastest, most exciting channel, and they frequently broach their boats to the current in executing various moves. The boats are filled with flotation to displace water in the event of a swamping or self-rescue.

Common maneuvers are:

- upstream ferries, peelouts and eddy turns
- paddling hard forward across the current and realigning to slip past obstacles
- surfing waves and sidesurfing in holes

As the maneuvers increase in difficulty, the paddlers play an increasingly calculated risk in pitting their skills against the power of the river. River running demands that a paddler be aware of hazards not always easily recognized and be able to avoid those dangers. These hazards are the most frequent killers:

- high water
- cold
- strainers
- dams, weirs, ledges, reversals, holes and hydraulics

Parallel Surfing

Side View

Top View

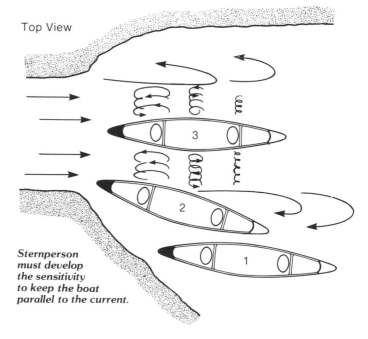

Sternperson must develop the sensitivity to keep the boat parallel to the current.

RESCUE

A primary concern of the American Canoe Association is safety in a sport that has potentially dangerous elements. While knowledge and skill help to minimize the dangers, risk cannot be eliminated completely in an adventurous activity.

Every paddler must be prepared to accept the consequences of an error in skill or judgment that leads to a swamped craft. Tipping over and swimming rapids are an integral part of canoesport. Paddlers must be prepared to accept the responsibility of rescuing themselves and, if possible, the rescuing of others.

A goal of paddling instruction is the education and training of participants in rescue techniques. Students should understand that each rescue situation is unique and usually requires one or more rescue techniques appropriate to a given situation. The development of the proper skills is a necessary part of a student's experience, and knowing a variety of rescue techniques is valuable.

But the first step is an awareness of procedures that can prevent the occurrence of a mishap in the first place.

Group Organization Helps to Prevent Problems

Each member of a paddling group (whether in a lesson or on subsequent trips) has specific responsibilities in the overall group organization to promote safety. While the group is collectively responsible for the conduct of a particular trip, participants are individually responsible for judging their qualifications to participate and in what manner.

Individuals may assume other responsibilities within a group to promote organization on the river.

The **lead craft** contains at least one experienced paddler with solid river reading skills. The paddler(s) in this boat:

- sets the pace and keeps track of group members to see if they are meeting the pace.
- selects the general course to be followed by other boats and communicates the route to other paddlers.
- scouts any rapids where a clear route isn't visible.
- carries extra equipment and rescue lines in the event that a rapid requires the set-up of shoreline rescue assistance.

The **sweep craft** is the last boat in the group and passes other craft only in the event of an emergency. The paddler(s) are experienced in rescue and often first aid. The sweep craft:

- carries spare gear, extra paddles and first aid equipment.
- keeps the group intact.

The remaining boats in the group have a responsibility to stay behind the lead boat and in front of the sweep boat. Any craft that inadvertently overtakes the lead boat, particularly in technical rapids, should stop as soon as it is possible to do so safely.

Other group responsibilities include:

- keeping the group compact to enhance organization.
- maintaining sufficient spacing to avoid collisions.
- keeping the next boat upstream in sight and stopping if it isn't visible.
- communicating messages to upstream and downstream boats.
- allowing a descending boat the right of way.
- avoiding crowded drops or eddies when no room exists for another boat.
- judging the difficulty of each rapid and the nature of participation and safety as the trip progresses.

AWA Universal River Signals

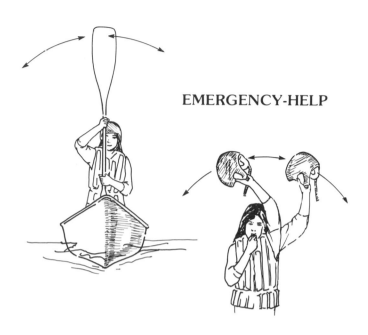

EMERGENCY-HELP

HELP/EMERGENCY: Assist the signaller as quickly as possible. Give three long blasts on a police whistle while waving a paddle, helmet or life vest over your head in a circular motion. If a whistle is not available, use the visual signal alone. A whistle can be carried on a lanyard, or attached to the zipper of a life vest.

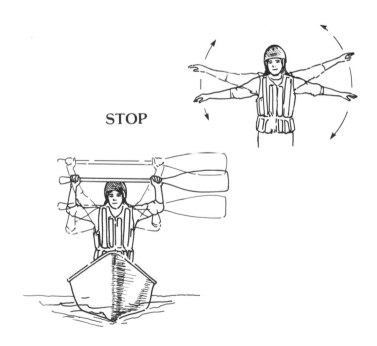

STOP

STOP: Potential hazard ahead. Form a horizontal bar with your paddle or outstretched arms. Move this bar up and down to attract attention by using a pumping motion with paddle or flying motion with arms. Those seeing the signal should pass it back to others in the party. Wait for "all clear" signal before proceeding, or scout ahead.

(Signals: continued on next page)

RUN CENTER

RUN THIS SIDE

RUN THIS SIDE

ALL CLEAR: Come ahead. In the absence of other directions, proceed down the center. Form a vertical bar with your paddle or with one arm held high above your head. Paddle blade should be turned flat for maximum visibility. To signal direction or a preferred course through a rapid around an obstruction, lower the previously vertical "all clear" by 45 degrees toward the side of the river with the preferred route. Never point toward the obstacle you wish to avoid.

ATTENTION

ATTENTION: This signal, audible only, consists of a series of short "chirps" on the police whistle. It is used where no emergency exists, but where the need to communicate is obvious and necessary. This signal should not be given casually; only when other common forms of communication are having little or no effect.

Group size is a consideration in river running. **The recommended minimum is three boats.** No one is encouraged to paddle alone.

The ACA's National Instruction Committee strongly suggests that certified instructors and competent aids maintain instructional units with the following staff/participant ratios. An instructional unit is the maximum class size for adequate service delivery and safety.

- Tandem flatwater courses — 10 participants with one certified instructor (10:1) or 20:2 if a competent aide (non-certified) is added to the teaching staff
- Tandem moving water and whitewater courses — the ratio is 10:2 (total number of boats is six)
- Solo classes (canoeing and kayaking) — the ratio is 4:1 or 8:2 with a competent aide

The committee suggests strongly that all solo moving water and whitewater courses be staffed with at least two instructors. (Head instructors should be certified.)

The recommendations are intended to promote safety and quality instruction for students through adequate supervision, because of the entry-level nature of ACA programs.

As the original group grows larger, paddlers should divide into two groups and reassign lead and sweep boats for each group.

Sufficient spacing between boats varies with the conditions. For flatwater paddling, a person generally remains within sight of the boats ahead of and behind his craft. In the event of variable or bad weather, paddlers are encouraged to stay within voice contact.

Spacing in whitewater is generally from 50 to 150 feet with the greater spacing recommended for more technical rapids. Each craft should give the downstream boat enough space so that a descending craft can maneuver around a broached boat. Boats should not overtake another craft in rapids.

Other factors are important in trip planning:

1. Select lakes and rivers with access points where shuttle or emergency vehicles may be parked. Additional first aid equipment, dry clothing and food can be stored at these points. Beginner paddlers may tire easily, and any paddler can be affected by cold weather and water and may need to stop early.

2. Advance scouting of rivers is prudent. Paddlers should check rivers on the same day of a proposed trip in the event of quickly-changing water levels. The *International Scale of River Difficulty* is a useful tool in selecting rivers. River guidebooks will describe river sections by the international scale and be helpful in matching a section's suitability to the skills of a particular group.

3. Well-thought-out route choices can help to prevent problems. A direct route across a large lake is a good choice during clear weather. But a more conservative route is better during bad weather, where bays and coves offer protection from wind. Traveling along the shore also enables a group to move during inclement weather.

4. On extended or remote trips, a group's plans and schedule should be filed with a responsible individual who will alert authorities if the group is overdue. Establishing rescue procedures and possible evacuation points can speed a rescue.

Rescue Priorities

Every paddler must understand rescue priorities to help reduce the confusion in rescue situations. Rescuers must avoid compounding a problem by becoming victims themselves. The priorities are:

- people
- boats
- equipment

1. *The first priority is a paddler in the water.* All rescue operations are based on the paddler's initiation of a self-rescue. A decked boater should recover from an upset with an Eskimo roll whenever possible. Paddlers should swim to safety immediately if imminent danger exists (strainers, hazardous rapids).

An integral component is a paddler's responsibility to a partner. If a paddler cannot see his partner, he must establish voice contact to insure that the other person is conscious, uninjured and beginning to self-rescue. Communication between partners is an essential element of effective rescue.

Experienced paddlers will usually instinctively self-rescue with their paddles in hand because of training and practice. Boats and other equipment are rescued only when it is safe to do so.

2. *The second priority is the swamped boat.* Paddlers should try to execute a self-rescue with the swamped boat if possible. The boat has flotation and is easily spotted by rescuers. However, if the weight and pressure of the boat inhibits safety or the ability to continue a self-rescue, they should leave the boat and swim to safety.

3. *The third priority is equipment.* On flatwater, equipment will float near the swamped craft, and gear bags will bob in the water until paddlers are safe and the bags can be collected. In whitewater, equipment gathers in eddies or along river bends for collection later.

Establishing rescue priorities helps to promote quick, efficient rescue. If all paddlers understand their responsibilities in a rescue operation, then the rescue can often be managed more effectively.

The Need for Immediate Action

After swamping, paddlers can suffer greatly from the effects of immersion. Rescues must be executed quickly to prevent immersion hypothermia. The numbing effects of cold water, even during the warm season, can inhibit the ability of paddlers to help themselves.

The best treatment for hypothermia is prevention, because the effects of cold water are potentially deadly. Water conducts heat away from a person's body 32 times faster than air. Physical activity like swimming causes people to lose heat even faster, because blood is pumped to extremities and cooled rapidly.

In cold water, swift rescue is essential before paddlers lose the ability to rescue themselves. A paddler's safety and well-being is a priority before the rescue of boats and equipment.

Emergency care manuals show that intense and uncontrolled shivering is an early sign of hypothermia. Loss of motor control (including slurred speech) and violent shivering will follow. As the body temperature drops, a person will appear increasingly confused and shivering will disappear. Eventually, loss of consciousness results and leads to drowning.

General Group Responsibilities in All Rescues

When a boat capsizes or swamps, all paddlers must evaluate the situation and determine a good course of action to rescue victims safely. Rescue situations can vary greatly, and the different nature of each incident determines which techniques are appropriate.

These general guidelines can help:

1. Alert other paddlers to the presence of victims in the water.

2. Swimmers initiate self-rescue procedures immediately and be ready to accept assistance from others.

3. Other paddlers assist in a rescue to the best of their abilities when it is safe to do so.

4. All paddlers not involved in assisting the swimmers stop as soon as they can safely do so, and they continue to evaluate the unfolding rescue in the event that their assistance is needed.

5. All paddlers should avoid converging on the rescue scene, because additional accidents may result.

Rescue skills require training and practice to execute them quickly and efficiently. As paddlers tackle lake trips of a remote nature and rivers of increasing difficulty, their skills should match the demands of the environment.

Flatwater Rescue

Swampings or capsizings on flatwater are often caused by wind, waves, powerboat wakes, improper trim and a paddler's poor balance. A paddler(s) can rescue a swamped craft in deep water without assistance from other boats. Several techniques can be valuable:

Self-Rescue

Capistrano flip. For open boats. Paddlers overturn the swamped boat completely and duck under it to come up in the air pocket.

In unison, the paddlers use a scissor kick to push the craft above the water surface and to roll it upright in the air. With more flotation to make the boat ride high in the water, the boat will be uprighted with less water in it. In boats with limited flotation, the canoe is often flipped and remains partially swamped.

Shake-outs. For open boats. Paddlers keep the swamped boat upright in the water, and one paddler pushes down on one end of the canoe as he pushes the boat forward. The end must be lifted before the water flows back in. An alternative is pushing down and away on one side and then pulling up on the gunwale before water flows back. With more shallow sides or less tumblehome, the boat will be uprighted with less water in it.

If these methods only partially empty the canoe of water, canoeists can still paddle the boat to shore. Progress may be slow and unbalanced, but the canoe can be paddled. Bailers can be used to empty the boat further.

A support party can also provide assistance.

Group Rescue

Boat-over-boat. For all boat types. A rescue boat paddles into position perpendicular to the swamped craft, while the swimming paddler moves to the opposite end of overturned boat. (If not already overturned, the boat needs to be flipped for water to drain from it.) Tandem paddlers move to opposite ends to assist. The rescuer lifts one end and pulls the craft across the mid-section of his boat, while the swimmer pushes down the far end to help break suction with the water. The tandem paddler nearest the rescuer helps to push the boat up.

The tipped craft is moved hand-over-hand across the rescue craft, until it is balanced, rolled upright and slid into the water. The boat is moved parallel to the rescue craft to help the paddler reenter the craft.

This **catamaran** stabilizes both boats so that paddlers can reenter without tipping over the boat again. A **trimaran** with three craft creates greater stability if needed. The paddlers in the third boat hold onto the rescue craft and enable the rescuer(s) to pull the swimmer into or onto their empty craft.

A "flatwater-style" boat-over-boat rescue is appropriate in river sections with calm pools or moving water with no obstructions.

All paddlers should communicate clearly during a rescue to reduce any confusion. Sometimes, newcomers to the sport need coaching to be effective self- or group rescuers.

Boat-over-Boat Rescue

1. Lift the overturned boat across the gunwales of the rescue boat. Swimmers should help if possible.

2. The rescuers roll the empty boat upright and stay low to maintain their balance.
3. Rescuers slide the upright boat into the water and position it next to the rescue boat. A catamaran helps to stabilize the empty boat while swimmers re-enter it.

Whitewater Rescue

Common causes of swamping or capsizing in whitewater are broaches, large waves, roiling cross-currents and a paddler's poor downstream lean during various maneuvers. Abrupt capsizings are often caused by the failure to provide adequate boat lean when entering an opposing current.

Unpremeditated spills are part of whitewater sports, and paddlers must be prepared to swim any rapid that they are about to descend.

Self-Rescue

Every paddler must actively self-rescue whenever possible. Paddlers improve their safety by:

1. never standing up in moving water, because deaths

have occurred from foot entrapments when the current pushes a paddler underwater.

2. keeping feet up near the surface of the water and kicking hard.

3. facing downriver with feet out in front to prepare to fend off oncoming obstacles.

4. keeping the buttocks elevated to slip over obstacles rather than bumping into rocks.

5. looking for an unobstructed shore and swimming directly to it when the route is free of obstacles. Use eddies between fast currents to get to shore.

6. swimming away from hazards, like strainers, holes, undercut rocks and the boat if downstream of it.

If a paddler is executing a self-rescue with a craft, the same guidelines apply to the situation. The paddler should consider several additional factors:

1. Get to the upstream side of the craft and grab the end of the boat nearest the safest shore. Hold onto the painter line or the grab loop. With open canoes, a paddler can hold the line several feet away from the boat for greater visibility of downstream obstacles.

2. Swim hard directly toward the safest shore, tugging the boat in a broached position if no obstacles exist.

3. In a rock garden, align the boat with the current to slip between obstacles. Once a clear section is reached, then swim with the boat to the safest shore.

4. Be aware of other paddlers who are preparing to assist.

Self Rescue

CURRENT DIRECTION

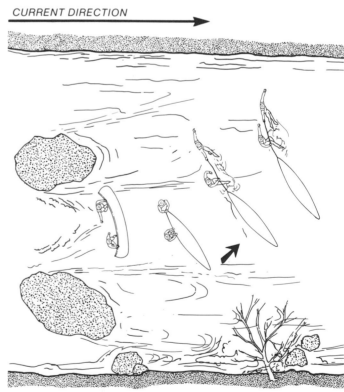

Paddlers should immediately begin an active self-rescue with their paddle and boat if possible. They should move quickly toward the safest shore.

Group Rescue

Group assistance in rescue is based upon the swimmer's initiation of self-rescue. Paddlers nearest the swimmer are often able to offer quick assistance, and they should determine the most effective type of assistance for that particular rescue situation.

All paddlers should analyze their actions to avoid further complications in the rescue. **Do not converge upon a rescue in process, if assistance is NOT needed.**

Group rescue techniques include:

Boat-assisted rescue. A rescuer(s) assumes an upstream ferry position above the swimmers who are performing self-rescue. The rescue boat swings into position so that the swimmers can grab the painter line or grab loop from the rescue craft. Then the rescuer(s) paddle hard to ferry the swimmers and the swamped craft to a safe shore.

An enormous pressure is exerted upon the swimmers who are stretched between the rescue craft and the swamped boat. If the swimmers cannot hold on to the boats, they should let go of the swamped craft which can be recovered later. The first priority is getting the paddlers to shore.

Bumping. A rescue craft paddles into position amidship of the swamped boat. A perpendicular angle will enable the rescue boat to bump the swamped canoe strongly without changing its ferry angle. Bumping works effectively with tandem open boats and kayaks because they provide the extra power to get the boat to shore quickly. A bump rescue is often performed in conjunction with a boat-assisted rescue.

Boat-Assisted Rescue With Bumping

CURRENT DIRECTION

Other paddlers can assist a swimmer who is performing a self-rescue. One rescue boat can tow the swimmer, while another can drive the capsized boat toward shore by bumping.

Eskimo Rescue. This rescue is used with decked boaters who are unable to perform an Eskimo roll. The rescue craft moves into position with its bow near the submerged paddler's hands. The hands should be above the water and in search of the rescue craft. The paddler uses the bow of the rescue craft to roll up. If the Eskimo rescue fails, then the paddler performs a wet exit and begins to self-rescue. The rescue craft can choose an alternative method of assistance at this point.

Shoreline Rescue. When a difficult rapid demands a solid safety system, paddlers experienced with throw lines or throw bags can provide assistance from shore. The ideal location for shoreline rescue is below the rapid in a river section that is relatively free of obstacles. Swimmers and swamped boats can swing into shore with less bumping into obstacles.

Paddlers use the ropes from ledges and rocks in the river when terrain dictates it (ie. a wide river), but unobstructed shorelines are often more effective.

The spacing of lines depends upon the current velocity and the shoreline area. Generally, paddlers station themselves far enough apart so that their lines will not tangle. The upstream line is thrown first, and the second or third lines are thrown in their respective order only if the previous throws are bad or the swimmer fails to grab one. The swimmer shouldn't be inundated with several lines.

If using throw bags, test the line before throwing it to make sure the coils feed out easily. If using a line, coil it properly so that it unwinds off the hand without tangling.

Practice with a line or bag to improve accuracy and distance of the throw. A good line is bright, floatable and thick enough to grab firmly.

When performing a throwline rescue:

1. Get the swimmer's attention.
2. Yell "rope" once the line is thrown accurately.
3. Aim for the swimmer or just downstream of the person, and throw past him. Use an underhand swing of the line similar to the throwing of a bowling ball.
4. Prepare to swing the swimmer into shore on the line or to change the person's position in the river (in the event of obstacles) by moving along the shore.

Rescuers should not wrap or coil the line around any part of their bodies, because the rope can tighten and drag a person into the water. If the rescuer needs the assistance of a belay to hold the line, then corresponding pressure is experienced by the swimmer who doesn't have the same advantage of a belay. The swimmer may be unable to hold onto the line. In that situation, the rescuer should move with the line to release the pressure, until he is able to find the next location to swing the paddler into shore.

Shoreline Rescue

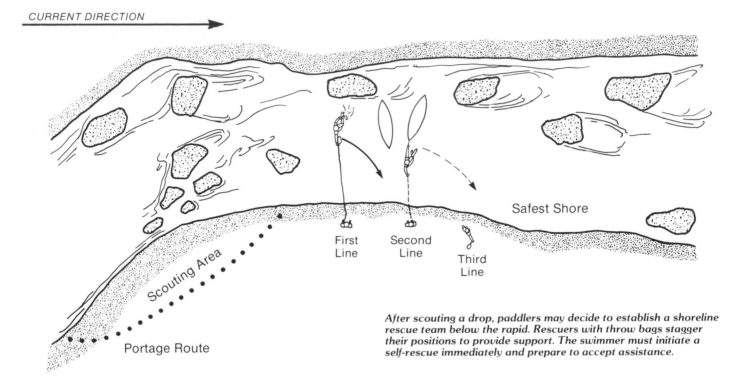

CURRENT DIRECTION

Safest Shore

First Line

Second Line

Third Line

Scouting Area

Portage Route

After scouting a drop, paddlers may decide to establish a shoreline rescue team below the rapid. Rescuers with throw bags stagger their positions to provide support. The swimmer must initiate a self-rescue immediately and prepare to accept assistance.

Rescuing a Pinned Craft

Once a craft is pinned against an obstacle, the water pressure exerted against the boat is often too severe for paddlers to recover the boat.

Mechanical assistance may be needed to overcome the force of the water. One common method for open boats is the **Steve Thomas rope trick,** while other mechanical advantages like a **Z-Drag** can work for all boats.

Instructors can find detailed descriptions and illustrations of mechanical rescues in more specialized publications. Rescue texts are available from the ACA Bookservice, and rescue workshops are often available from local paddling schools and clubs. Mechanical rescues require practice of knot and rope skills as well as the specific mechanical system.

Note: illustrated on following page.

How To Rescue A Broached Canoe
...also known as "The Steve Thomas Rope Trick"
originally published as a Safety Service of COASTAL CANOEISTS
reprinted by permission of illustrator Les Fry

R. Steve Thomas, Jr., of Hopewell, Virginia is quick to disclaim originating this rescue technique. But Coastal Canoeists who have seen him in action regard him as the system's most experienced practitioner.

Rather than dismember a canoe by pulling out one thwart at a time, this rescue system pulls on the entire boat at once—the gunnels, thwarts, and hull.

Stated simply, it helps the canoe roll, dump itself, come up empty. The trick is getting the line in the proper position to do the most good (and the least damage). The more quickly the rescue can be effected, the better are the chances of success.

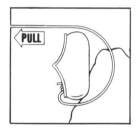

If your boat ever gets broached on an obstruction — open side upstream...

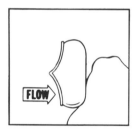

This is the do-it-yourself method (with a little help from your friends) to set it free.

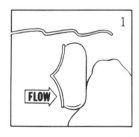

Climb up on the rock behind (downstream of) the canoe. Catch the line as the rescue party heaves it from upstream.

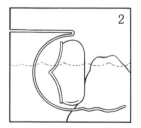

Get a good firm grip on a bight of the line. Forcefully throw a wad of about 8 or 10 feet of its running end into the water on the upstream side and let it flush under the canoe.

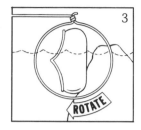

Pick up the running end as it comes through to the downstream side and tie it to the bight. Any knot that won't slip will serve, but the less bulky the better.

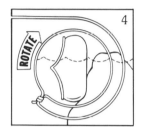

Rotate the knot around the DOWNSTREAM side of the canoe and back up the front side to where you can reach it.

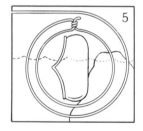

Untie the knot and release the RUNNING end, holding the bight. Pull whichever side of the bight will draw the now free running end through...

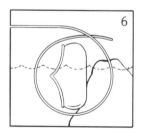

...to the front side. (The experienced rescue party will take up any slack in the line to keep it from swirling around the legs.)

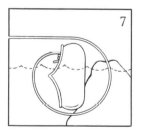

Tie the running end to the thwart (or seat frame) nearest the obstruction that's holding your canoe. Use any hitch or knot that will hold, but tie it in a loose loop.

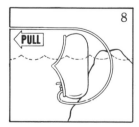

Slide the loop to the bottom of the thwart and the rescue party PULLS. The canoe should roll upstream and pop to the surface almost empty. (If a second line can be secured nearer one end of the canoe and pulled from a different direction, it may help prevent the canoe's washing back down on the same obstruction or one even worse.)

Emergency Management Planning: A Responsible Approach

Prevention is the premise of emergency management, where the safest approach is taking measures that prevent accidents, injuries and medical emergencies.

Training is the First Step. All paddlers should be committed to continuing education to upgrade their skills and to remain prepared for handling emergencies properly. Training and practice are important components of prevention-oriented paddling.

Paddlers should develop skills in rescue, first aid, emergency care and evacuation procedures. The standard in adventurous activities today is that paddlers be knowledgeable and able to perform in these four major areas.

Knowledge of Rescue Techniques is the Second Step. Teaching river safety and rescue skills is an important part of every paddling program. Paddlers need to transfer those skills to paddling experiences beyond a formal instructional program.

Advance Preparation for Medical Emergencies

All participants should advise instructors of any medical considerations that could affect their participation, such as:

1. chronic conditions that can affect athletic performance (allergies, disorders and physical handicaps)
2. temporary conditions that affect performance (recent illnesses and injuries)
3. medication that affects muscular coordination, mental acuity and judgment

Participants with allergies that may cause problems should carry their medication during the program or trip. Paddlers with recent illnesses or injuries should keep instructors or group leaders informed of their mental and physical condition.

Organizations may ask participants to note their swimming ability on the medical form as a means of determining a person's comfort level in and on the water.

First-aid kits are important during any phase of the program. Waterproof kits can be tied easily into boats for river trips. The kit is a good place for emergency phone numbers (local police, rescue squads and hospitals).

Paddlers should know the general area near the river for several reasons:

1. to inform state police of an injured party's exact location if an ambulance is being dispatched.
2. to drive injured or ill participants to the local hospital if needed. (Listing the hospital addresses is a good idea.)

A group's itinerary should be left with a sponsoring organization, including an estimated time of return. An agency is apprised of a problem in the event that the group fails to return on time.

Medical Response to an Accident

Accidents can be difficult situations for many paddlers.

Paddlers unfamiliar with injuries or medical emergencies often react adversely to the tension created by an accident. Particularly if the victim is a relative or friend, paddlers can disrupt rescues or medical care already under way.

An injured person is the first priority, and paddlers should try to rescue the victim without complicating the injury when possible.

Paddlers should assess the nature of injuries and determine the emergency-care procedures that suit the situation. Two situations usually develop: 1) care of the injured person(s) and 2) care of other paddlers.

Trained medical providers or paddlers with knowledge of first aid immediately administer medical care to the victim(s). They may need assistance from other paddlers who should be standing by to help.

Other paddlers who are not involved with medical care can rescue boats and equipment **when it is safe to do so.** Unsafe retrieval of equipment can compound the situation by causing additional accidents.

Evacuation

An injured or ill person may need to be evacuated. Familiarity with the region helps in determining the quickest or safest point of evacuation. A knowledge of local roads, suitability of terrain for evacuation and nearby inhabited buildings is also helpful in the event of an accident.

Evacuations can be difficult and fatiguing because of demanding terrain. The physical and psychological welfare of a group is enhanced by staying together, keeping warm and remaining occupied, if possible. A clear plan of action communicated to all group members is essential.

If the group needs to continue downriver to a suitable evacuation point, a different group organization may be necessary:

1. The injured person may need to be paddled to the take-out.
2. Extra boats and gear may be stored at the site, or qualified paddlers are assigned to tow the boats or paddle solo.
3. New lead and sweep boats should be established clearly.
4. A new route may be scouted to continue downriver.

If messengers leave the scene to obtain help, they should travel in pairs and, if possible, have the following information for rescue assistance:

1. details of the nature of the accident and signs and symptoms of the injury
2. money for pay phones (in first aid kit)
3. emergency phone numbers for assistance
4. knowledge of the exact location of the injured person(s)

If the group is divided during evacuation proceedings, each smaller group should understand the intended plan of the other party. The evacuating party should make arrangements for the transport of the remaining group.

After the Accident or Evacuation

Paddlers should review the incident to discuss questions and concerns. Groups often have a need to analyze accident situations and to express their feelings about the experience.

Injured parties often need the help of other paddlers in analyzing the events and in resolving questions surrounding the incident.

Some organizations require that an instructor or trip leader complete an accident report on the same day that the incident occurred. Prompt completion helps the person to remember the incident clearly and to fill out the form with specific details.

The ACA collects and distributes accident information in an attempt to prevent similiar accidents in the sport.

ACA COURSES

Suggested content outlines for American Canoe Association courses are included in this chapter. The content is outlined by the various types of craft at three basic levels of instruction:

1. flatwater
2. moving water
3. whitewater

At the end of each outline, the recommended strokes for that level of course are listed. The National Instruction Committee does not require that every stroke on this comprehensive list be taught.

The needs and abilities of students will determine the number and type of strokes to be introduced at each level. Some strokes have similar functions, but the mechanics of their execution are different. The selection of suitable strokes for students often depends upon their strength, flexibility and psychological comfort. For those reasons, the NIC also does not differentiate between "beginner" and "intermediate" strokes.

This chapter also addresses changes in the format of instructor courses. The recommended content is outlined for the following courses:

1. instructor certification
2. methods workshops
3. instructor trainer updates

The outlines are designed to provide a foundation for instructors to develop programs that promote safe, enjoyable paddling and that reflect the most up-to-date information in canoesport. The content is deliberately flexible to accommodate the diversity of paddlers across the United States. The ACA understands that instructors will tailor their programs to meet the needs of individuals in their region.

Registration Procedures for Courses

Certified instructors should register their courses with the ACA National Office. The *Basic Workshop Registration Form* should be filed three weeks prior to the workshop, and can also be used to request insurance coverage. To receive credit for teaching, the *Basic Workshop Report Form* must be filed upon completion of the course.

Liability Insurance for Courses

The ACA liability insurance program is offered to all certified instructors who are paid or volunteers, administrators, officials, coaches or member clubs and who conduct their programs in accordance with ACA guidelines. It is not a substitute for commercial business insurance. All instructors requesting insurance must be governing members.

The policy is a third-person general liability policy that currently provides the named insured with up to a million dollars of coverage for bodily injury or property damage claims. The claims must arise from ACA-sanctioned functions or activities.

To obtain insurance, the fees must be paid before the class begins.

Many of the ACA's activity committees also offer sanctioning and insurance to ACA members. In these cases, the sanctioning must come from the divisional representative on the particular committee or the vice-commodore of the division (primarily for divisional events). The fee structure is different for these events.

Contact the National Office for further information: Suite 1900, P.O. Box 1190, Newington, Virginia 22122.

FLATWATER COURSE

Note: This content outline for a flatwater program applies to all types of craft. Specific strokes for each craft are listed at the conclusion of the outline.

Instructor Qualifications: This course may be taught by ACA instructors currently certified in flatwater, moving water or whitewater.

Minimum Duration of Course: 16 hours

Recommended Staffing: Tandem 10:1 with certified instructor — 20:2 with certified instructor and competent aide Solo 4:1 with certified instructor — 8:2 with certified instructor and competent aide

Locations: Sheltered lake, pond or swimming pool

Course Outline:

I. Introduction to Paddling
  A. Types of Paddling
    1. Flatwater — Lakes and Rivers
    2. Whitewater
    3. Touring
    4. Racing — Marathon
    5. Racing — Olympic "High Kneel"
  B. Equipment
    1. Personal Clothing and Gear
    2. Boats — Parts and Design
    3. Paddles — Parts and Design
    4. Accessory Equipment — First Aid and Rescue Gear
  C. Orientation to Safety
    1. Basic Safety Considerations
    2. Basic Hazards on Flatwater
  D. Transportation of Boats
    1. Carrying Methods
    2. Car Top Tie-Downs
    3. Trailer Tie-Downs
  E. Orienting the Paddler to the Boat
    1. Balance and Trim
    2. Basic Stances — Sitting, Kneeling
    3. Entries and Exits — From Land, From Water

II. Introduction to Paddling Technique
  A. Modern Paddling Theory
    1. Biomechanics of Paddling — Efficient Use of Body
    2. Stroke Mechanics — Laws of Motion

III. Introduction to Paddling Strokes
  A. Parts of a Stroke
    1. Propulsion
    2. Recovery
  B. Types of Strokes
    1. Power
    2. Turning
    3. Bracing
  C. Stretching and Warm-ups

IV. Calm-water Practice of Maneuvers
  A. Spins
  B. Sideslips
  C. Bracing
  D. Straight Forward
  E. Straight Reverse
  F. U-Turns or Landings

V. Rescue
  A. Principles of Rescue
    1. Rescue Priorities — People, Boats, Gear
    2. Responsibilities of Victim
    3. Responsibilities of Rescuers
  B. Types of Rescue
    1. Self-Rescue
    2. Capistrano Flip
    3. Boat-over-Boat Rescue
    4. Catamarans and Trimarans

VI. Flatwater Trips
  A. Group Organization
  B. Route Finding

VII. Recommendations for Practice
  A. ACA Programs
  B. Paddling Clubs
  C. Training Camps — Olympic
  D. Individual Evaluations

Specific Strokes for Flatwater Programs

Tandem Canoe (OC-2, C-2)

Forward	Stationary Draw
Back	Cross Stationary Draw
"J" Stroke	Forward ¼ Sweep
Draw	Reverse ¼ Sweep
Cross Draw	Stationary Pry
Duffek	High Brace
Cross Duffek	Low Brace

Solo Canoe (OC-1, C-1)

Forward	Cross Stationary Draw
Back	Forward ½ Sweep
"J" Stroke	Reverse ½ Sweep
Draw	Stationary Pry
Cross Draw	High Brace
Duffek	Low Brace
Cross Duffek	C-Stroke
Stationary Draw	

Kayak (K-1)

Forward	Forward Sweep
Back	Reverse Sweep
Draw	High Brace
Duffek	Low Brace
Stationary Draw	

MOVING WATER COURSE

Note: This content outline applies to moving water programs for all types of craft. Specific strokes for different craft are listed at the conclusion of the outline.

Instructor Qualifications: This course may be taught by ACA instructors currently certified in moving water or whitewater.

Minimum Duration of Course: **24** hours

Recommended Staffing: Tandem 5:1 with certified instructor — 10:2 with certified instructor and competent aide Solo 4:1 with certified instructor — 8:2 with certified instructor and competent aide

Locations: Flatwater
Moving Water - Classes B and C

Course Outline:

I.   Introduction to Paddling
   A. Types of Paddling
     1. Flatwater — Lakes and Rivers
     2. Whitewater
     3. Touring
     4. Racing — Marathon, Olympic, Slalom, Downriver
   B. Equipment
     1. Personal Clothing and Gear
       Cold Weather/Cold Water Protection
     2. Boats — Parts and Design
     3. Paddles — Parts and Design
     4. Safety Equipment — Flotation and Outfitting
     5. Rescue Equipment — First Aid and Gear
   C. Orientation to Safety
     1. Basic Safety Considerations in Moving Water
     2. Basic Hazards on Moving Water
   D. Transportation of Boats
     1. Carrying Methods
     2. Car Top Tie-Downs
     3. Trailer Tie-Downs
   E. Orienting the Paddler to the Boat
     1. Balance and Trim
     2. Basic Stances — Sitting, Kneeling
     3. Entries and Exits — From Land, From Water

II. Introduction to Paddling Technique
   A. Modern Paddling Theory
     1. Biomechanics of Paddling — Efficient Use of Body
     2. Stroke Mechanics   Laws of Motion

III. Introduction to Paddling Strokes
   A. Parts of a Stroke
     1. Propulsion
     2. Recovery
   B. Types of Strokes
     1. Power
     2. Turning
     3. Bracing
   C. Stretching and Warm-ups

IV. Calm-water Practice of Maneuvers
   A. Spins
   B. Sideslips
   C. Bracing
   D. Straight Course Forward
   E. Straight Course Reverse
   F. U-Turns (for Eddy Turns and Peelouts)

V.   Moving Water Practice
   A. Ferries — Upstream and Downstream
   B. Eddy Turns
   C. Peelouts
   D. Sequences of Maneuvers — S-turns
   E. Self-Rescue
   F. Group Rescue

VI. River Reading
   A. Fundamentals of River Currents
     1. Characteristics of Current — Downstream V's, Eddy lines, etc.
     2. Effects of Obstacles — Ledges, Strainers, etc.
     3. Hazards — Holes, Dams, etc.
     4. International Scale of River Difficulty
   B. River Reading Responsibilities
     1. General Course
     2. Immediate Course
     3. Individual Responsibilities
     4. Problems — Broaches, Pinnings, etc.

VII. River Running
   A. Individual Responsibilities
   B. Strategies in Running Rivers
   C. Group Organization on the River
     1. Lead and Sweep Boats
     2. AWA River Signals System
   D. Trip Planning Considerations

VIII. Rescue
   A. Principles of Rescue
     1. Rescue Priorities — People, Boats, Gear
     2. Responsibilities of Victim
     3. Responsibilities of Rescuers
   B. Effects of Immersion Hypothermia
   C. Types of Rescue
     1. Self-Rescue
     2. Boat-over-Boat Rescue
     3. Boat-Assisted Rescue (Towing)
     4. Bumping
     5. Eskimo Rescue
     6. Catamarans and Trimarans
     7. Shoreline Rescue
     8. Pinned Craft

IX. Recommendations for Practice
   A. ACA Programs
   B. Paddling Clubs
   C. Training Camps
   D. Individual Evaluations

Specific Strokes for Moving Water Programs

Tandem Canoeing (OC-2, C-2)

Cross Forward	Shallow-Water Draw
Slice "J"	Reverse "J"
Pryaway	Turning Braces
Shallow-Water Pry	

Solo Canoeing (OC-1, C-1)

Cross Forward	Shallow-Water Draw
Slice "J"	Reverse "J"
Pryaway	Turning Braces
Shallow-Water Pry	

Kayaking (K-1)
Turning Braces

Plus strokes listed under the flatwater program.

WHITEWATER COURSE

Note: This content outline applies to whitewater programs for all types of craft. Specific strokes for different craft are listed at the conclusion of the outline.

Instructor Qualifications: This course may be taught by ACA instructors currently certified in whitewater.

Minimum Duration of Course: **32** hours

Recommended Staffing: Tandem 5:1 with certified instructor — 10:2 with certified instructor and competent aide Solo 4:1 with certified instructor — 8:2 with certified instructor and competent aide

Locations: Flatwater
Moving Water - Classes B and C
Whitewater - Class 1 and Class II

Course Outline:

I. Introduction to Paddling
  A. Types of Paddling (Canoeing and Kayaking)
    1. Flatwater — Lakes and Rivers
    2. Whitewater
    3. Touring
    4. Racing — Marathon, Olympic, Slalom, Downriver
  B. Equipment
    1. Personal Clothing and Gear
       Cold Weather/Cold Water Protection
    2. Boats — Parts and Design
    3. Paddles — Parts and Design
    4. Safety Equipment — Flotation and Outfitting
    5. Rescue Equipment — First Aid and Gear
  C. Orientation to Safety
    1. Basic Safety Considerations in Whitewater
    2. Basic Hazards on Whitewater
  D. Transportation of Boats
    1. Carrying Methods
    2. Car Top Tie-Downs
    3. Trailer Tie-Downs
  E. Orienting the Paddler to the Boat
    1. Balance and Trim
    2. Basic Stances — Sitting, Kneeling
    3. Entries and Exits — From Land, From Water

II. Introduction to Paddling Technique
  A. Modern Paddling Theory
    1. Biomechanics of Paddling — Efficient Use of Body
    2. Stroke Mechanics — Laws of Motion

III. Introduction to Paddling Strokes
  A. Parts of a Stroke
    1. Propulsion
    2. Recovery
  B. Types of Strokes
    1. Power
    2. Turning
    3. Bracing
  C. Stretching and Warm-ups

IV. Calm-water Practice of Maneuvers
  A. Spins
  B. Sideslips
  C. Bracing

D. Straight Course Forward
E. Straight Course Reverse
F. U-Turns (for Eddy Turns and Peelouts)

V. Moving Water Practice of Maneuvers
  A. Ferries — Upstream and Downstream
  B. Eddy Turns
  C. Peelouts
  D. Sequences of Maneuvers — S-turns
  E. Self-Rescue
  F. Group Rescue

VI. River Reading
  A. Fundamentals of River Currents
    1. Characteristics of Current — Downstream V's, etc.
    2. Effects of Obstacles — Ledges, Holes, etc.
    3. Hazards — Strainers, Dams, etc.
    4. International Scale of River Difficulty
  B. River Reading Responsibilities
    1. General Course
    2. Immediate Course
    3. Individual Responsibilities
    4. Problems — Broaches, Pinnings, etc.

VII. River Running
  A. Individual Responsibilities
  B. Strategies in Running Rivers
  C. Group Organization on the River
    1. Lead and Sweep Boats
    2. AWA River Signals System
  D. Trip Planning Considerations

VIII. Rescue
  A. Principles of Rescue
    1. Rescue Priorities — People, Boats, Gear
    2. Responsibilities of Victim
    3. Responsibilities of Rescuers
  B. Types of Rescue
    1. Self-Rescue
    2. Boat-over-Boat Rescue
    3. Boat-Assisted Rescue (Towing)
    4. Bumping
    5. Eskimo Rescues
    6. Catamarans and Trimarans
    7. Shoreline Rescue
    8. Pinned Craft

IX. Recommendations for Practice
  A. ACA Programs
  B. Paddling Clubs
  C. Individual Evaluations

Specific Strokes for Whitewater Programs

Tandem Canoeing (OC-2, C-2)

Compound Back	Cross Back
Far Back	Cross Low Brace
Pryaway	Reverse Duffek

Solo Canoeing (OC-1, C-1)

Compound Back	Cross Back
Far Back	Cross Low Brace
Pryaway	Reverse Duffek

Kayaking (K-1)
Turning Braces and Duffek refinements

Plus strokes listed under the flatwater and moving water programs.

Instructor Certification Workshops

A New Approach to the Certification Process

The National Instruction Committee has revised its recommended format for certification programs to offer candidates a greater opportunity to excel. The committee has based its approach upon programs adopted by other certifying bodies, such as Professional Ski Instructors of America.

The changes include:

1. Three levels of certification (flatwater, moving water and whitewater)
2. Three areas of evaluation (technical knowledge, teaching skills and paddling skills)
3. An emphasis on numerous "mini" teaching presentations rather than longer lecture-style presentations
4. An emphasis on small-group organization within the total group so that each instructor trainer may examine candidates more effectively

The new format divides the certification process into three consecutive levels: flatwater, moving water and whitewater. A candidate for certification must pass at each level before proceeding to the next one. It gives candidates an opportunity to obtain certification at whatever level their abilities merit.

The NIC advises instructor trainers to begin the program with the evaluation for flatwater certification (20 hours), then the moving water evaluation (8 hours) and, finally, the whitewater evaluation (8 hours). The total program should be at least 36 hours long.

The new format provides a clearer process for evaluating candidates in the three areas: technical knowledge, teaching skills and paddling skills. They learn at the end of each level whether they passed or failed *and in what area(s)*. They should be given specific suggestions for improvement in problem areas.

The change allows the instructor trainers to dismiss people who are not qualified to advance to the next level. It also satisfies the needs of advanced paddlers to perform at a higher level without the hindrance of less-skilled paddlers. Those people who are not invited to attempt the next level of certification can be offered a separate program designed to improve their skills and to prepare for a subsequent certification program.

The new format also emphasizes a structure where candidates are given numerous non-threatening opportunities to demonstrate their abilities more fully. These opportunities are shorter in duration, often a minute to five minutes, for three reasons: 1) to reduce the pressure upon a candidate to "perform" with the result that they deliver relaxed, higher quality presentations, 2) to increase the number of opportunities available to candidates to demonstrate skills so that their chances of success increase, and 3) to vary the types of situations where candidates demonstrate skills to offer a wider variety of chances for success.

A change is recommended in the organization of the group. When the number of candidates exceeds five people (the recommended ratio of students to an instructor), the instructor trainer should divide the participants into smaller groups. Assign an instructor trainer or IT candidate to each group. Candidates generally perform better in smaller groups, and the small group size offers the instructor trainer a closer look at each candidate for a better evaluation. The small groups remain the same throughout the program, and the instructor trainers change between the groups in order to be able to evaluate each candidate.

Instructor trainers are also discovering the benefits of offering a certification course in two sessions. In the first one, candidates become acquainted with the requirements for certification and the evaluation process. They also obtain specific feedback on areas of strength and weakness in order to prepare for the second session. A period of several weeks between sessions often allows paddlers to prepare for passing the final certification, if they failed to enter the first session with the necessary skills.

Administrative Requirements for Certification

An instructor must:

1. be at least 18 years old
2. successfully complete an instructor training workshop
3. become an ACA member (Associate or Governing)

To maintain certification, an instructor must:

1. teach two courses that meet ACA standards in a four-year period and report the courses with the ACA national office
2. attend once in four years at least one of the following: an instructor training workshop, a divisional methods workshop or assist in teaching an instructor training workshop
3. maintain ACA membership (Associate or Governing)

Proficiency Requirements in Certification

Candidates must be able to demonstrate their proficiency in technical knowledge, paddling and teaching at each specific level.

Technical knowledge includes a general knowledge of canoesport, safety, equipment, conditioning, paddling theory, river reading, river running strategies and rescue.

Teaching skills include logistics, lesson organization, class control, teaching of specific technical topics, technique analysis and demonstration of leadership skills and judgment. Awareness of a variety of teaching methods is urged.

Paddling skills include an ability to model efficient technique and to rescue paddlers and capsized boats. Specific skills vary between levels:

Flatwater candidates should be good models of flatwater skills and maneuvers.

Moving water candidates should be competent Class I paddlers and be able to demonstrate control in Class II water. Closed boaters should have a reliable roll.

Whitewater candidates should be competent Class II paddlers and be able to demonstrate control in Class III water. Closed boaters should have a reliable roll.

Certification Courses

Note: Each program outline is listed by level of certification (flatwater, moving water, whitewater). The outline applies to the three types of paddling (open canoeing, decked canoeing and kayaking) at that level.

Instructor Trainer Qualifications: The instructor trainer must be currently certified in the specific type of craft being used and at the appropriate level of instruction (flatwater, moving water, whitewater).

FLATWATER CERTIFICATION

Minimum Duration: **24** hours
Locations: Flatwater

Course Outline:

I. The Certification Process
   A. Review Levels of Certification
      1. Flatwater
      2. Moving Water
      3. Whitewater
   B. Review Proficiency Requirements for Certification
      1. Technical Knowledge
      2. Teaching Skills
      3. Paddling Skills
   C. Review Administrative Requirements for Certification
   D. Explain Evaluation Process
      1. Assignment of Formal Teaching Topics —
         5-Minute and 10-Minute Presentations
      2. Outline of Informal Teaching Opportunities

II. The Learning Process
   A. Learning Theory
   B. Barriers to Learning
   C. Characteristics of an Effective Instructor
   D. Teaching and Demonstrating Methods

III. Technical Knowledge (to be covered through candidate's "Formal Teaching Topics" — see Appendix B — and instructor trainer presentations)
   A. Knowledge of Canoesport in General
   B. Equipment — Flatwater Craft
      1. Recreational
      2. Competitive
   C. Clothing
   D. Safety Considerations
   E. Modern Paddling Theory
      1. Recreational
      2. Competitive
   F. Strokes
   G. Maneuvers
   H. Rescue
      1. Self
      2. Group
   I. Group Organization
   J. Route Finding on Lakes
   K. Legal Liability in Adventure Education

IV. Teaching Skills (use "mini" presentations)
   A. Flatwater Stroke Demonstrations
   B. On-land Presentations (of above topics)
   C. On-water Teaching (of above topics)

V. Paddling Skills
   A. Ability to Model Technique
   B. Ability to Execute Rescues

VI. Videotape Review, if possible
   A. Teaching Presentations
   B. Paddling Skills

VII. Final Meeting
   A. Written Evaluations
   B. Oral Evaluation
   C. Participant Critique of Course
   D. Awarding of Certificates on Individual Basis
   E. Review of Continuing Education Requirements

MOVING WATER CERTIFICATION

Minimum Duration: **32** hours (when combined with flatwater certification)

Locations: Flatwater
Moving Water

Course Outline:

I. The Certification Process
   A. Review Levels of Certification
      1. Flatwater
      2. Moving Water
      3. Whitewater
   B. Review Proficiency Requirements for Certification
      1. Technical Knowledge
      2. Teaching Skills
      3. Paddling Skills
   C. Review Administrative Requirements for Certification
   D. Explain Evaluation Process
      1. Assignment of Formal Teaching Topics —
         5-Minute and 10-Minute Presentations
      2. Outline of Informal Teaching Opportunities

II. The Learning Process
   A. Learning Theory
   B. Barriers to Learning
   C. Characteristics of an Effective Instructor
   D. Teaching and Demonstrating Methods

III. Technical Knowledge (use of "mini" presentations)
   A. Knowledge of Canoesport in General
   B. Equipment
      1. Recreational
      2. Competitive
   C. Clothing
   D. Safety
   E. Modern Paddling Theory
      1. Recreational
      2. Competitive
   F. Strokes
   G. Maneuvers
   H. Rescue
      1. Self
      2. Group
   I. Group Organization
   J. Route Finding
      1. On Lakes
      2. On Rivers
   K. River Reading
   L. River Running
   M. Legal Liability in Adventure Education

IV. Teaching Skills (use "mini" presentations)
   A. Moving Water Stroke Demonstrations
   B. On-land Presentations (of above topics)
   C. On-water Teaching (of above topics)

V. Paddling Skills (at practice sites, on river trips)
   A. Ability to Model Technique (in flatwater through Class I current)
   B. Ability to Execute Rescues (in moving water)

VI. Videotape Review, if possible
   A. Teaching Presentations
   B. Paddling Skills

VII. Final Meeting
   A. Written Evaluations
   B. Oral Evaluation
   C. Participant Critique of Course
   D. Awarding of Certificates on Individual Basis
   E. Review of Continuing Education Requirements

WHITEWATER CERTIFICATION

Minimum Duration: **40** hours (when combined)
with flatwater and moving
water certification)
Locations: Flatwater
Moving Water
Class I-III rapids

Course Outline:

I. The Certification Process
    A. Review Levels of Certification
       1. Flatwater
       2. Moving Water
       3. Whitewater
    B. Review Proficiency Requirements for Certification
       1. Technical Knowledge
       2. Teaching Skills
       3. Paddling Skills
    C. Review Administrative Requirements for Certification
    D. Explain Evaluation Process
       1. Assignment of Formal Teaching Topics —
          5-Minute and 10-Minute Presentations
       2. Outline of Informal Teaching Opportunities

II. The Learning Process
    A. Learning Theory
    B. Barriers to Learning
    C. Characteristics of an Effective Instructor
    D. Teaching and Demonstrating Methods

III. Technical Knowledge (use of "mini" presentations)
    A. Knowledge of Canoesport in General
    B. Equipment
       1. Recreational
       2. Competitive
    C. Clothing
    D. Safety
    E. Modern Paddling Theory
       1. Recreational
       2. Competitive
    F. Strokes
    G. Maneuvers
    H. Rescue
       1. Self
       2. Group
    I. Group Organization
    J. Route Finding
       1. On Lakes
       2. On Rivers
    K. River Reading
    L. River Running
    M. Legal Liability in Adventure Education

IV. Teaching Skills (use "mini" presentations)
    A. Whitewater Stroke Demonstrations
    B. On-land Presentations (of above topics)
    C. On-water Teaching (of above topics)

V. Paddling Skills (at practice sites, on river trips)
    A. Ability to Model Technique (in flatwater through
       Class III water)
    B. Ability to Execute Rescues (in Class II water)

VI. Videotape Review, if possible
    A. Teaching Presentations
    B. Paddling Skills

VII. Final Meeting
    A. Written Evaluations
    B. Oral Evaluation
    C. Participant Critique of Course
    D. Awarding of Certificates on Individual Basis
    E. Review of Continuing Education Requirements

Methods Workshops

The instructor methods workshop is designed to provide certified instructors with an opportunity to refresh their skills in paddling and teaching. The workshop also provides instructors with an update of changes in American Canoe Association policy and course content.

An instructor is required to attend a methods workshop once in four years.

Instructor Qualifications: The methods workshops are coordinated by National Instruction Committee divisional representatives and at least one certified instructor trainer.

Minimum Duration: 12 hours
Locations: Classroom setting
Flatwater
Moving Water
Class I-III rivers, depending upon certification level of participants

Course Outline:

I.   Orientation to ACA
    A. Update on ACA Policies and Administration
    B. Update on NIC Policies and Administration

II. Teaching Skills
    A. Review of Modern Paddling Theory
    B. Sharing of Teaching Methods
        1. Strokes
        2. Maneuvers
        3. Technical Subjects

III. Paddling Skills
    A. Refinement of Personal Paddling Style
    B. Refinement of Demonstration Skills

IV. Related Practice
    A. Rescue
    B. Other Craft New to the Instructor

V.   Final Meeting
    A. Comments/Opinions on ACA Programs/Policies (to be forwarded to NIC)

Instructor Trainers

Within each regional division, instructor trainers conduct the instructor certification workshops and the methods workshops. They are responsible for the training of prospective instructors and the evaluation of instructor candidates for the three levels of certification. Through the methods workshops, they provide the most important link in the continuing education of certified instructors. An instructor trainer must be aware of the most current paddling skills, teaching methods and technical knowledge accepted in canoesport.

Any certified instructor can request that he or she be considered for instructor trainer status in any of the three disciplines: open canoeing, decked canoeing and kayaking. The candidate is selected by a committee of three certified instructors, including at least one instructor trainer. The candidate must co-lead an instructor certification workshop with the instructor trainer. At the completion of the workshop, the instructor trainer submits a letter of recommendation for the candidate to the chairperson of the National Instruction Committee.

Proficiency Requirements for an Instructor Trainer

The candidate should demonstrate superior qualities in the same areas as instructor candidates: paddling skills, teaching skills and technical knowledge. In the area of teaching skills, the candidate should demonstrate an ability to train other people as instructors.

Administrative Requirements for an Instructor Trainer

The candidate must:
1. be 21 years of age
2. be an ACA governing member
3. be a certified instructor for no less than two years
4. attend an instructor trainer update at least once every four years
5. organize, teach and report any four courses (flatwater, moving water, whitewater and instructor certification workshop) in a four-year period

Reinstatement of Instructor Trainer Status

An instructor trainer whose status has lapsed must:
1. be an ACA governing member
2. attend an instructor trainer update
3. demonstrate proficiency in paddling skills, teaching methods and knowledge of current guidelines for all ACA courses to the satisfaction of the National Instruction Committee chairperson or to a committee of one instructor trainer and two instructors

Instructor Trainer Updates

The instructor trainer updates will be conducted annually or more frequently to provide continuing education for instructor trainers. The chairperson of the National Instruction Committee or a designee will determine the location and schedule of various updates.

The content of the updates is based upon the instructor certification course outlines and the methods workshop outline. The intent is to share current information on canoesport and to develop further skills for training prospective instructors.

ACA Instructors as Prudent Professionals

The dramatic rise in the popularity of canoesport is good news for the paddling world, but the trend raises concern about safety in the sport — with good reason. The probability of accidents has risen with the increased popularity of paddling. Every paddler is familiar with the sight of unknowledgeable boaters careening through rapids, often *without lifejackets* and *with alcohol* in the boats. But another scenario is the one where paddling programs may involve unreasonable risks.

Paddling is an activity with an element of danger, and it's a major reason why people are attracted to the sport. With the proper training, experience and judgment, paddlers can manage the risk inherent in the sport. That issue should be a relevant one for instructors who are helping students develop those skills. Instructors must face the fact that the public is expecting instructional programs that do not place them in an unreasonably risky situation. They need to be prudent professionals in their instructional programs, regardless of whether they are paid or volunteer instructors.

This section outlines the basic issues surrounding an instructor's legal liability in adventurous activities. It addresses the underlying components of litigation when a party alleges that reasonable safety precautions were *NOT* followed in a paddling activity that led to an accident and injury

A Charge of Negligence

Negligence is the basis of almost *every* charge against an instructor of outdoor activities. Such a charge points to the failure of the instructor to do what a reasonable, prudent person would normally do under those circumstances. An instructor is expected to provide a *standard of care* worthy of a reasonable, prudent professional who knows the best practices and current techniques in the profession. Negligence may also be charged for the instructor's performance of something that a reasonable, prudent person would *NOT* have done under the circumstances.

An instructor's negligence must have *caused* the injury, and *proximate cause* is the crux of the claim to be proven by the injured participant. The injured person must show that the instructor had a duty to provide a safe environment, that he or she violated that duty and that the violation caused the accident.

The injured person must then prove that the injury was *foreseeable* to the instructor and that the instructor could forsee that his or her actions might cause damage. How is proof or evidence of this negligence shown in the courtroom?

Testimony by witnesses is the primary method, and witnesses can be *fact* or *expert*. Fact witnesses testify to what they saw, felt and heard — which can be the injured party or other people who were involved in the incident. Thus, how an instructor's performance is viewed by other people in a workshop is vitally important. The expert witness is a person who, by training and experience, has greater knowledge in the specific field than the general population. In this case an instructor's performance is addressed in terms of standards that are accepted by other experts in the field.

An Instructor's Defense

Instructors must defend their actions by showing that they were reasonable and represented good teaching practices. Certification is to the paddling instructor's benefit, because it shows that the instructor has made an effort to become educated by obtaining knowledge from experts in the field. But instructors must also show that they acted in accordance with the teaching methods endorsed by those experts. By using American Canoe Association guidelines, the instructor can base his classes upon a well-thought-out program of activities that helps participants to build solid skills.

In a suit, the instructor must address the issue of whether a participant's own actions might have caused or contributed to the accident. The instructor is trying to show a cause between the participant's performance or judgment and the injury. In addition, the instructor is trying to prove to the jury that the participant should have foreseen that injury might result from his actions.

The claim that the instructor is a volunteer rather than a paid professional is *NOT* a defense. A volunteer instructor is just as liable as a paid employee leading an activity. The crux is that the person assumes the mantle of leadership and performs the functions of that role.

Specific Problems Leading to Negligence Claims

The *adequacy of supervision* is usually questioned, because good supervision can help to prevent unnecessary accidents. Instructors should maintain constant supervision during the entire program.

The court requires proof of the foreseeable presence of *general danger* and that a competent instructor has moved to prevent an accident. The belief is that the general situation would lead to an accident, if it were left unsupervised.

Direct supervision implies more adequate supervision, and for that reason, the ACA recommends that its instructors use controlled settings such as river practice sites to develop skills safely. *Indirect supervision* implies less adequate supervision, such as river trips where boats are spaced along the river and not directly under the instructor's supervision. River trips are acceptable only when the paddlers' abilities warrant a river experience, and they want to accept the challenge.

Listed are specific suggestions that can improve the quality of supervision:

1. Be thoroughly familiar with current standards in the activity.

2. Establish safety procedures and insure that they are followed.

3. Follow a *written* plan of activities. Their written nature is legal evidence of an instructor's preparation.

4. Do not leave a group unsupervised, ie. permitting paddling practice while you are running a shuttle.

5. Direct the activity so that *every* participant is within sight.

6. If directed by a supervisor to teach an acitivity beyond your abilities, inform the person of your limited abilities and improve your competency.

The instructor should anticipate hazards in the activity and help to promote the well-being of participants, including the provision of good quality, well-maintained safety equipment. Specific suggestions include:

1. Outlining safety considerations in the activity so that each person can take active responsibility for himself and, if possible, others.

2. Providing safety equipment and acquainting students with their responsibility to use it.

3. Modifying an activity to avoid unreasonable risks.

Selection of activities is an important consideration. The instructor should select a program of activities that is appropriate to the age, size and skill level or participants. The activities should be geared to the abilities of the least skilled member of a group. Students should be encouraged to keep the instructor informed of how they view their progress.

The condition of facilities and equipment should be examined carefully for hazards. A personal inspection of equipment is best, and students should not use equipment in disrepair.

Poor judgment is a difficult area to assess, but instructors can consider the following suggestions:

1. Never ask a participant to perform an unreasonably dangerous task.

2. Be well-trained in the most current first aid procedures.

3. Establish a written list of emergency procedures with emergency numbers in the event of an accident.

4. Certain risks are a part of paddling, but an instructor should choose activities where the risks are well-thought-out and reasonable.

5. Choose activities within the guidelines of a recommended curriculum. It is difficult to explain an accident that occurs in an activity outside established guidelines.

6. Avoid mismatched partners in activities where physical performance is important. Match participants by size, weight and ability.

The important of *communication* cannot be overlooked, because participants must be aware of the dangers in the activities. It is to the instructor's benefit to prove that a participant was informed of the dangers and then knowingly ignored them. No person can assume the risk of dangers of which he may be unaware and may not appreciate.

Students leave a paddling lesson with new skills and techniques that they need to practice, and they are enthusiastic about the varied opportunities that allow them to continue their involvement in the sport. Most people like to paddle canoes and kayaks as relaxing outdoor recreation. Some intend to explore remote wilderness rivers and lakes. Others are intrigued by paddling competition and are interested in racing as the ideal outlet for their competitive instincts.

Instructors need not be competitors themselves, but they should be familiar with all aspects of competition and be ready to share this information with their students. Racing is rising in popularity and attracting new paddlers, because many local and regional events offer an easy and rewarding introduction. "Open" and "citizen's" classes are filled with newcomers to paddling competition. Racing offers an excellent avenue for recreational paddlers to refine and test their skills. Interest in national and international racing is also growing as American paddlers become a stronger presence in competition.

Canoesport features an exciting array of opportunities for flatwater and whitewater racing: marathon, slalom, downriver, poling, sailing, ocean kayaking and flatwater sprints. The styles, skills and techniques are different for each sport, and individuals will vary in their commitment to training and competition.

Involving new paddlers is important to the continued development of racing, and an instructor can help with the process. Interested students do want to learn basic racing skills and techniques in their lessons. They look to instructors to help them understand the relationship between recreational and racing styles of paddling. The relationship is a strong one in recent years.

Recreational paddlers and racers share a common desire to paddle *efficiently* despite their differences in styles. The fastest racers are often the ones who paddle most efficiently, and recreational paddlers are studying the racers increasingly to improve their own techniques. Those improvements have changed recreational instruction in recent years, and instructors can look to competitors for more changes in the future.

Types of Competition

The choices in competition seem endless: flatwater or whitewater; canoes or kayaks; solo, tandem or foursome; women's, men's or mixed; downriver or slalom; paddles or poles.

But those classifications still aren't specific enough in canoesport because a tremendous number of additional choices exist! Boats are the best example. Their hull configurations dictate whether they are "short, medium or long;" a "competition cruiser" or a "pro boat." Distances can also vary greatly, and racers can opt for short sprints or longer endurance events. Five, 15, 50 or 500 miles? It's the competitor's choice.

The variety may be confusing to a newcomer, but it benefits paddlers by offering numerous opportunities for their participation. Interested paddlers can choose an event that suits their abilities. Or even better, they can begin with shorter or easier events to test their skills before they graduate to longer or harder events. A look at the different types of competition can help a person to choose.

The "At A Glance" summaries for each discipline are adapted from *canoe* magazine's *Spectator's Guide.*

Marathon

Marathon racing has venerable roots as a native American sport practiced by Indians and Inuit on inland lakes and open seas. Its colorful past is present in modern-day competition; the events are as varied as ever.

Marathon racing generally refers to distance events longer than five miles that challenge a paddler's endurance. But no upper limit or standard exists for the longest distances, and some events feature "ultra" marathon distances of approximately 250 miles. Competition can take hours or days. Multi-day "stage" races, overnight events and inclusion in triathlons are just a sampling of the types of marathons.

Marathons are generally divided into three major categories: 1) a small branch closely related to Olympic flatwater that leads to international competition through the International Canoe Federation; 2) "pro boat" racing which evolved from the Canadian voyageurs and allows only one set of boat specifications and a tandem team only; and 3) the largest series of marathon events which is run through the United States Canoe Association.

The USCA recognizes 10 championship classes and a host of other classes, including juniors, masters (40 years and older), "super aluminum," families and more. As a result, marathon racing offers a mix of intense and low-key events, and it's one of the largest and most popular competitive activities in paddling.

Racers adopt a "switch style" of paddling, where they alternate paddling sides frequently. In a tandem team, the pace is set by the bow paddler while the stern paddler calls the switches. Timing with the switches is crucial to maintain speed and keep the boat on a straight course. Most paddlers use bent-shaft paddles for more efficient short power strokes.

Many marathons require portages in the midst of the course, often around dams, and paddlers find themselves sprinting down city streets or through the woods with the boat on their shoulders.

Marathon At A Glance

Governing Body: United States Canoe Association for national races (since 1968 when it left the ACA) and the ACA for all International Canoe Federation races.

Distances: five to 500 miles (no standards); the USCA recommends races of 15 to 20 miles (two or three hours).

Scoring: Fastest elapsed time from start to finish line.

Format: Generally point-to-point on flatwater or moving water; mass starts (unless lack of space dictates heats); classes may have separate or combined start times (ie. women may be started before men).

Classes: Open: no seeding. USCA: men's C-1, C-2; women's C-1, C-2; mixed C-2, ACA/ICF; men's and women's C-1 and C-2; men's K-1, K-2.

Equipment: Specific hull configurations for major marathon classifications with limits on water line widths, bow and stern height, overall hull lengths and decking lengths. (See *Chapter V: Equipment*)

Restrictions: No rudders.

Information: USCA, P.O. Box 5743, Lafayette, IN 47904

Olympic Flatwater

Americans have been involved in Olympic flatwater competition since the 1924 Games when both sprints and distance events were included. Since then, long distance events have been dropped from the Olympics but are retained in the World Championships.

The sprints challenge a paddler's ability to power quickly across short distances. Speed is the primary consideration, strokes are shorter and the stroke rate is high, especially in the final sprint to the finish line. These 500- and 1,000-meter courses take just a few minutes to cover.

As the distances lengthen, paddlers alter their training to increase their endurance. The men race a 10,000-meter course (6.2 miles), while women cover 5,000 meters.

Olympic boats are designed for straight-ahead speed, and they tend to have rounded, tippy hulls. Canoeists use a "high kneel" position that creates more instability and requires delicate balance. The paddler rests on one knee in the boat, and the tandem teams must coordinate their balance and timing to paddle powerfully in unison.

The two- and four-person kayaking events are a favorite of spectators, because the teams paddle in perfect synchronization with their double-bladed paddles. The power generated by a K-4 can tow a water skier, and the speed at which the boat travels is inspiring.

Olympic Flatwater At A Glance

Governing Body: American Canoe Association through its National Paddling Committee for U.S. events; International Canoe Federation for international events.
Distances: Sprints, 500 and 1,000 meters. Distance, 5,000 and 10,000 meters.
Scoring: Elapsed time from start to finish line.
Format: Sprints, point-to-point with different heats and nine boats in separate lanes; three top finishers from each heat go to the semi-finals; rest of heat go to a "repecharges" for a second chance to reach semi-finals. Distance races, a mass start on a course that circles 1,000 meters.
Classes: Men's K-1, K-2 and K-4 and C-1, C-2, Women's K-1, K-2 and K-4. Only ranked paddlers selected for Olympic competition.
Equipment: Boats must meet ICF specifications.
Restrictions: Riding waves (surfing) illegal in sprints and permitted in 10,000-meter races.
Information: NPC Office, U.S. Olympic Complex, 1750 E. Boulder St., Colorado Springs, CO 80909.

Open Boat Whitewater

Open canoe racing is an exciting endeavor where paddlers battle Class II-III whitewater to negotiate a course quickly. Waves, holes, fast eddies and chutes are obstacles that paddlers must handle successfully without shipping water into their boats.

Competition helps aspiring recreational paddlers to develop their skills in many areas. They must read the river accurately to choose the fastest course, and their judgment must be solid, particularly the timing of specific maneuvers as they race along the course.

Two major events exist: downriver and slalom. Downriver events cover longer distances from eight to 25 miles, and they require more endurance training from participants. Many competitors are also marathon racers, because the training is applicable to both events and the racing schedules are complementary. Few whitewater events are scheduled after the spring season when water levels drop, and paddlers can extend their racing season through marathon events in the summer and fall.

The downriver boats — long and narrow — track easily so that paddlers can concentrate on hard forward paddling. They are less tippy and more maneuverable than flatwater marathon boats so that paddlers can negotiate rock gardens.

Slalom events are shorter events, where a gates course stretches along a quarter-mile of river. Racers must negotiate the various gates in a forward or reverse boat position, depending upon the configuration of the poles. (The red pole is always to the left of the paddlers.)

Precision paddling is necessary to avoid hitting the poles. The gates in an open boat slalom course tend to be slightly wider apart than closed boat courses, because open canoes are unable to slip under the poles.

Boat design has changed dramatically to enable the canoes to pivot quickly. These highly-maneuverable craft are more like closed boats, and as a result, many open boat racers also race closed boats.

Gates courses are used increasingly in recreational paddling classes to teach boat control and to improve timing of maneuvers. These training areas are used by racers and recreational paddlers alike, because the current is mild enough to paddle back upriver and repeat the course.

Open Boat Whitewater At A Glance

Governing Body: American Canoe Association through its Whitewater Open Canoe Division.
Distances: Slalom, 20 to 30 gates on Class II-III whitewater over a quarter mile. Downriver, eight to 25 miles on Class II-III.
Format: Interval starts by classes. Combined time from two runs.
Scoring: Slalom, elapsed time plus penalties for missed gates (50 seconds) and touches (5 seconds). Downriver, elapsed time.
Equipment: PFDs and helmets required. "Short" canoes are at least 12 feet, "medium" at least 15 feet, tandem at least 15 feet.

Closed Boat Whitewater

Intensify the whitewater, change to decked boats, and a different type of competition emerges — closed boat whitewater. These events are an exciting spectacle on very difficult whitewater. Racers are highly skilled in negotiating courses that demand quick decision-making and advanced maneuvers.

Canoeists and kayakers race in these events, and the C-1 paddlers are extremely close to the kayakers with their times. The American decked canoeists are a world power after winning recent World Championships, and the excitement surrounding their success has been good for competition within the country. At local and regional levels, paddlers are increasingly interested in closed boat racing.

It is similar to open boat racing in its offerings. Downriver and slalom are the two major events, although some downriver races are called "wildwater" when the course contains more Class III-IV water. The downriver events are usually 3.6 to 7.2 miles of flat-out speed through rapids. A good course often contains at least one well-known drop that will win or lose the race for competitors, depending upon how well they handle the water at high speeds.

The slalom courses are tighter than open boat competition, since decked boats can "sneak" gates by slipping underneath them. The course usually requires a series of powerful, intricate moves to negotiate gates without touching the poles. Course times are often two to three minutes, and winning times can be as close as a hundredth of a second.

The intensity varies along the race course, but spectators can count on sections where competitors must surf across holes, spin in rolling waves and "jet" ferry across chutes.

Many local clubs, organizations or outfitters offer less intense courses, usually when water levels begin to subside in the summer. These events are an excellent introduction for new racers to develop racing strategies and a "feel" for negotiating courses.

Closed Boat Whitewater At A Glance

Governing Body: American Canoe Association through its National Slalom and Wildwater Committee.

Distances: Slalom, 25 gates over a distance of 800 meters on Class III (90 percent) and IV water. Downriver, point-to- point along at least a three-kilometer course, usually six to 12 kilometers (3.6 to 7.2 miles) on Class I-II water. Wildwater may contain Class III-IV water.

Scoring: Slalom, same as open boat whitewater, best time of two runs. Downriver, elapsed time.

Format: Interval starts by classes. Open competitions, ranked paddlers may be run after unranked paddlers (seeding required only at team selection trials).

Classes: Men's K-1, C-1 and C-2. Women's K-1 (C-1 and mixed C-2 in national competition only).

Poling

Poling a canoe is a fascinating endeavor, and many canoeists became interested in its merits to avoid lengthy shuttles! A canoe can be poled up and down a river whether it's a turbulent Calss II-III stretch or a shallow stream. Poling allows people to park their cars at the put-in and return to the same spot.

Canoeists stand in their boats and use a long pole (often as long as the craft) to push off the river bottom. Paddlers experienced in poling can use the pole just like a paddle. They execute eddy turns and peelouts in a similar fashion, although their standing position adds a significant challenge. Balancing the canoe is a skill learned after an initial period spent lurching about in the boat.

Competition which involves upriver and downriver moves is governed by the American Canoe Association through its National Poling Committee.

Triathlons

The triathlon has become a prominent sports event in recent years, and paddling is an integral part of many triathlons. Spring events often feature whitewater downriver legs, while summer events include a flatwater marathon section. Teams or solo competitors enter these relay competitions, and the majority are recreational or "citizen's" racers.

The United States Canoe Association sanctions a triathlon series with these recommended distances and order: Total, 50 kilometers (30 miles); Canoe, 12 kilometers (7.2 miles); Bike, 30 kilometers (18 miles); Run, 8 kilometers (6 miles).

Local clubs and organizations also sponsor triathlons, and the races often deviate from the USCA standards. Late winter events can include skiing and paddling. These local events attract an enthusiastic following of skilled and inexperienced racers.

The American Canoe Association, a proud tradition of service...

For more than a century, the American Canoe Association (ACA) has remained committed to its straightforward mission: to promote safe and enjoyable canoeing and other paddlesport activities. Founded in 1880, the ACA has grown from a small fraternal organization into the national governing body for canoeing and kayaking. America's oldest and largest national non-profit paddlesports organization and one of the nation's oldest sporting organizations of any kind, the ACA represents some 35,000 members and affiliates across the country.

In striving to address its mission over the years, the ACA has continually expanded its activities and programs. The association's instruction program is an excellent example. Continually upgraded to keep pace with new skill development and changing equipment and techniques, the program sets training and certification standards for a nationwide cadre of canoe and kayak instructors and instructor trainers. Its goal: to provide safe and wholesome sport and recreation for the estimated 17 million Americans who paddle each year.

Today, new challenges face the ACA. The skyrocketing popularity of recreational paddling has moved canoeing and kayaking near the top of a list of the fastest-growing recreational activities in America. Among the priorities of the ACA are:

• Working in partnership with the U.S. Coast Guard to develop state-of-the-art safety materials and programs.

• The Paddle FREE program, designed to assure paddlers access to recreational waterways and to preserve those rivers, lakes and streams as a part of a quality environment.

• Development of new outreach programs to serve a variety of special populations. Included are programs for those who normally would be unable to experience the benefits and enjoyment of paddling because of physical or economic disadvantages.

• Fostering athletic competition by sanctioning a nationwide series of races in disciplines including flatwater sprint, decked boat slalom and wildwater, whitewater open canoe racing, marathon, judged freestyle and super distance racing.*

• Serving local clubs through a variety of services including clinics, cruises and informational programs.

ACA members receive a number of additional benefits. Included are six issues of *Paddler* magazine each year, *The American Canoeist*, the association's regular newsletter listing activities and other information of interest to members, and use of the ACA's private island in Canada's St. Lawrence Islands National Park.

The American Canoe Association is a fully qualified 501(c)(3) corporation, governed by its members through a system of twelve regional divisions and through committees established to assure representation in areas of paddling ranging from mainstream recreation through competition, including such varied interests as canoe sailing, poling and interpretive sport paddling.

For further information or to join the ACA, contact:

The American Canoe Association
7432 Alban Station Blvd., Suite B-226
Springfield, VA 22150
(703)451-0141

*In order to best serve the highly specialized interests of Olympic athletes, the ACA has delegated the responsibility for the Olympic paddling programs to the U.S. Canoe and Kayak Team.

APPENDIX

Formal Teaching Topics
ACA Instructor Certification Workshops

Prospective instructors can deliver a 5-minute presentation to a *beginner* audience on one of the following topics. The intent is to summarize important points that an instructor might mention to participants at the outset of a workshop. The assignment is intended to be open-ended. The nature of the material and the method of delivery is the candidate's choice, but the presentation should be **concise.**

1. Basic Orientation to Canoesport
2. Basic Orientation to Safety in Paddling

Prospective instructors can also deliver a 10-minute presentation to a *beginner* audience on one of the following topics. The method of delivery is the candidates' choice, and they should edit their material for a concise presentation.

1. Safety on Large Bodies of Water
2. Group Safety on the River
3. Personal Clothing and Equipment
4. Boat Outfitting Techniques
5. Rescue Equipment
6. Fundamentals of River Currents
7. Ferries
8. Eddy Turns and Peelouts
9. Self-Rescue
10. River Features
11. Scouting Rapids
12. Playing Rock Gardens
13. Parallel and Side Surfing
14. Broaching Prevention and Recoveries
15. Boat-Assisted Rescue
16. Shoreline-Assisted Rescue
17. Group Organization on Rivers and Lakes
18. Dangers of Cold Water Paddling
19. Ethics and River Etiquette

Alternative topics can be assigned for delivery to an audience of *instructors.* These 20-minute presentations can address the following issues:

1. Legal Liability in Paddling
2. Emergency Management Planning for Paddling
3. Trip Planning
4. First Aid Preparedness in Water Environments

Notes